AF882268

Financing State-Owned Enterprises

AN OVERVIEW OF NATIONAL PRACTICES

OECD
BETTER POLICIES FOR BETTER LIVES

This work is published on the responsibility of the Secretary-General of the OECD. The opinions expressed and arguments employed herein do not necessarily reflect the official views of the OECD or of the governments of its member countries.

This document and any map included herein are without prejudice to the status of or sovereignty over any territory, to the delimitation of international frontiers and boundaries and to the name of any territory, city or area.

Please cite this publication as:
OECD (2014), *Financing State-Owned Enterprises: An Overview of National Practices*, OECD Publishing.
http://dx.doi.org/10.1787/9789264209091-en

ISBN 978-92-64-20899-5 (print)
ISBN 978-92-64-20909-1 (PDF)

The statistical data for Israel are supplied by and under the responsibility of the relevant Israeli authorities. The use of such data by the OECD is without prejudice to the status of the Golan Heights, East Jerusalem and Israeli settlements in the West Bank under the terms of international law.

Corrigenda to OECD publications may be found on line at: *www.oecd.org/about/publishing/corrigenda.htm*.

© OECD 2014

You can copy, download or print OECD content for your own use, and you can include excerpts from OECD publications, databases and multimedia products in your own documents, presentations, blogs, websites and teaching materials, provided that suitable acknowledgment of the source and copyright owner is given. All requests for public or commercial use and translation rights should be submitted to *rights@oecd.org*. Requests for permission to photocopy portions of this material for public or commercial use shall be addressed directly to the Copyright Clearance Center (CCC) at *info@copyright.com* or the Centre français d'exploitation du droit de copie (CFC) at *contact@cfcopies.com*.

Foreword

This report provides an overview of national policies and practices towards state-owned enterprise (SOE) financing in OECD and other countries. It summarises the decision-making processes surrounding SOE financing at different stages in the corporate life cycle, including as regards capital structure, rate-of-return requirements, dividend pay-outs and the provision of state support. It also takes stock of the main sources of SOE financing, and any mechanisms in place to ensure such financing is obtained on competitive conditions compared with private businesses.

The report is part of the ongoing work of the OECD Working Party on State Ownership and Privatisation Practices on The State in the Marketplace. It is related to earlier work on competitive neutrality, which examined practices to create a level playing field between state-owned and private companies when they compete in the commercial marketplace. The report draws primarily on a questionnaire-based exercise to which 22 countries contributed. The report was given final approval and declassified by the Working Party in December 2013. It was prepared by Korin Kane of the Corporate Affairs Division of the OECD Directorate for Financial and Enterprise Affairs, with guidance and input from Hans Christiansen.

Table of contents

Tables

Boxes

Preface by Rintaro Tamaki, Deputy Secretary-General, OECD

State-owned enterprises (SOEs) are important actors in the global economy. Some countries have many SOEs. In others, SOEs are less prevalent but operate in sectors of strategic importance such as public utilities. Sound financial governance of SOEs means better fiscal management and more efficient resource allocation in the broader economy. Policy makers come under growing pressure to ensure that SOEs create value for their owners who are, ultimately, the taxpayers and the broader public.

Beyond the national level, SOEs' expanding presence in the global marketplace has given rise to heightened concerns regarding the conditions of SOE financing and their impact on the competitive landscape. Some high-profile corporate takeovers featuring SOEs have triggered allegations of concessionary financing by their government owners. The issue of ensuring market-consistent financing conditions for SOEs was first addressed by the OECD in a 2012 report on maintaining a level playing field between state-owned and private businesses consistent with the standards set by the *OECD Guidelines on Corporate Governance of State-Owned Enterprises.*

This second report offers new information and greater clarity about how governments and SOEs make decisions regarding SOE financing. It offers practical, step-by-step information on how decisions are made relating to SOEs' capital structure, rate-of-return requirements, dividend pay-outs and state subsidies. It also examines the conditions attached to state capital infusions as well as commercial and state loans, showcasing useful practices for maintaining market-consistent financing terms. While it finds that a number of OECD countries have made important steps to professionalise the financial management of commercial SOEs, the report also identifies some persisting challenges that need to be tackled in order to bring practices more in line with comparable private companies. These include ensuring that rates-of-return and state capital infusions are market consistent, and neutralising advantageous commercial loan terms caused by perceived or implicit state guarantees.

I am confident that many of the practices outlined in the report will be a useful resource for policy makers looking to improve the financial governance of SOEs. The OECD stands ready to continue working with member and partner countries to exchange experiences on SOE governance reform and maximise SOEs' contributions to growth, development and prosperity.

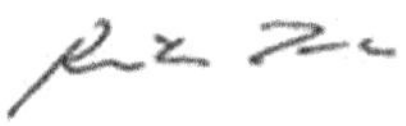

Rintaro Tamaki
Deputy Secretary-General, OECD

Executive summary

This report summarises national practices with respect to financing state-owned enterprises (SOEs) in 22 OECD and partner country delegates to the OECD Working Party on State Ownership and Privatisation Practices. Focusing on SOEs operating on a primarily commercial basis, the report provides an overview of how decisions are made regarding SOE financing, notably as regards capital structure appropriateness, rates-of-return, dividend pay-outs and subsidisation. It also takes stock of the main sources and forms of equity and debt financing for SOEs and examines whether such financing is obtained on market-consistent terms.

Capital structure: Policy and implementation

Determining an optimal capital structure. In most countries, capital structure decisions are the purview of SOE boards and management, with the authorities exercising varying degrees of oversight, including (i) limited government involvement; (ii) the provision of clear guidelines for identifying an appropriate capital structure; and (iii) direct review and approval. In countries with the highest level of capital policy elaboration, the authorities communicate an announced credit rating target, which is then used as a benchmark for all subsequent decisions impacting capital structure (rate-of-return requirements, dividend pay-outs, recapitalisations, etc.). Many countries that do not elaborate overarching capital structure guidelines do so implicitly via rate-of-return and/or dividend targets, as described below.

Establishing rate-of-return requirements. Establishing appropriate rate-of-return requirements can be challenging when SOEs are engaged in both commercial and non-commercial activities, especially if their costs are not structurally separated. In a majority of countries, SOEs are subject to explicit rate-of-return requirements, ranging from broad governmental guidelines applicable to all SOEs, to yearly targets elaborated for individual companies jointly by boards and the government. Some challenges remain, notably in assessing their comparability to private sector rates-of-return.

Setting dividend levels. Excessive dividend pay-outs can threaten the commercial viability of SOEs, while lower-than-market dividend levels can put SOEs at an undue financial advantage compared with their private competitors. Ensuring that dividend levels are a function of commercial performance, and not public policy or political objectives, is key to maintaining a level playing field between state-owned and private firms. In most countries, the authorities elaborate some form of dividend policy or target for SOEs, taking three main forms: (i) broad governmental guidelines; (ii) targets communicated as a percentage of net income; and (iii) (as discussed above) an overarching policy linking dividend levels to a target credit rating consistent with an industry benchmark.

Providing direct state support. Maintaining a level playing field does not mean that SOEs should not receive state support. Providing adequate compensation for any public service obligations is important to ensure SOEs are not at a commercial disadvantage *vis-à-vis* private competitors. However, state support for SOEs should be calibrated to the additional cost associated with the related public service obligation. This can be challenging in the absence of structural separation between commercial and public policy activities. In the majority of countries, state support for SOEs is provided, usually in compensation for public service obligations. Although EU state aid rules prohibit the provision of state support for anything other than public service obligations, the enforcement of these rules may be difficult to implement in practice.

Sources and conditions of SOE financing

Recapitalising SOEs. To maintain competitive neutrality, the conditions of SOE recapitalisations from the public budget should be consistent with private sector practices. In most countries where SOE recapitalisations from the public budget occur, the authorities have not put in place mechanisms to ensure market consistent equity costs. EU state aid rules do require that governments only inject capital if private investors in like circumstances would have acted similarly. However, compliance may be difficult to assess in practice. In only a handful of countries, the authorities communicate explicit requirements that public sector capital injections to SOEs must demonstrate a minimum expected return on investment, together with detailed methodologies for assessing compliance.

Financing through debt. In the majority of countries, SOEs access debt financing uniquely on the commercial marketplace. Commercial loans are by far the most prevalent form of debt financing, with a few large SOEs also issuing tradable debt securities. In a minority of countries, SOEs can (or must) access debt financing from the state treasury.

Identifying the cost of debt financing. In the majority of countries, SOEs do not benefit from standing government guarantees on their commercial debt. However, examples abound of specific SOEs – notably those providing public services – that do benefit from such guarantees. Although it is difficult to empirically assess the terms of commercial loans to SOEs, credit ratings and other indicators suggest that commercial lenders perceive implicit state guarantees for SOEs and price their loans accordingly. Only one country (Australia) has put in place a "debt neutrality charge" to compensate. The only other cases where mechanisms are in place to ensure market-consistent loan terms occur for a small number of specific SOEs that access debt financing directly from state institutions.

Remaining challenges to competitive neutrality

Many OECD governments approach SOE financing with a high degree of professionalism, bringing them closer to commonly agreed financial governance standards. This contrasts with the experiences of previous decades, whereby SOEs in a number of countries were used either (i) as revenue sources for the government, thus threatening their commercial viability or (ii) to house excess fiscal reserves, leading to over-capitalisation and poor public resource management. However, challenges remain, particularly for SOEs faced with the dual objectives of achieving commercial returns and delivering public services. The report identifies the following areas of particular concern:

- *Rates-of-return.* Although SOEs in a number of countries are subject to explicit rate-of-return requirements, it is difficult to assess whether they are comparable with those imposed on private enterprises, especially in cases where there is no structural separation between the commercial and non-commercial activities of SOEs.
- *Recapitalisation.* Only a minority of countries have put in place mechanisms to ensure that SOE recapitalisations take place on market-consistent terms. Most EU countries are subject to state aid rules prohibiting the provision of state subsidies for purposes other than public service. However, the enforcement of such rules can be difficult to implement in practice.
- *Perceived state guarantees.* Although only a few governments offer explicit guarantees on SOE debt, credit ratings and other indicators suggest that commercial lenders nonetheless perceive an implicit state guarantee, and price their loans accordingly. Only one country imposes a "debt neutrality charge" to compensate for this cost advantage.

1. Introduction

About this report

This report was developed in response to a request by the OECD Working Party on State Ownership and Privatisation Practices to take stock of national approaches to funding and financing of state-owned enterprises (SOEs) in OECD and partner countries. The exercise takes place in the context of the Working Party's work stream on "The state in the market place" and constitutes a follow up to its joint work with the OECD Competition Committee on competitive neutrality.

The purpose of the report is twofold. First, it seeks to shed light on how financing decisions are made regarding SOEs and to synthesise national policies and practices in this regard. Secondly, it examines a broad range of financial transactions and conditions which might make the cost of operating SOEs materially different than for private competitors, and identifies whether any mechanisms are in place to neutralise such differences.

The information is based primarily on responses to a questionnaire sent to OECD and partner countries, as well as follow up questions and interviews. In total, 22 countries responded to the questionnaire: Australia, Canada, Chile, Czech Republic, Estonia, Finland, Germany, Hungary, Ireland, Israel, Italy, Japan[1], Korea, Lithuania, the Netherlands, New Zealand, Norway, Poland, Slovenia, Sweden, Switzerland and the United Kingdom. The report summarises questionnaire responses and supplementary information received by end December 2013. Responses have been supplemented with additional research from publically available sources.

Scope and content

Good financial governance of SOEs is key to ensuring that they create value for their owners and, ultimately, that they contribute to an efficient allocation of capital resources in the broader economy. In financial terms, value creation occurs when the returns on a company's invested capital exceed its cost, i.e. when the net profits generated by a company's activities exceed the returns required by its providers of capital (lenders, owners and shareholders). In the case of SOEs, correctly identifying capital costs and their associated returns can be a challenge, particularly for SOEs with the dual objectives of operating profitably in a commercial marketplace and delivering public services. In such cases, if there is no clear structural separation between the two types of activities, it is difficult to distinguish between an SOE's purely commercial returns and the social (or public policy) returns on their non-commercial activities, as well as the respective costs associated with each activity.

Whether SOE financing comes from the public purse or the marketplace, ensuring that it is provided on market-consistent terms is key to maintaining a level playing field with private competitors. On the one hand, if SOEs can finance their operations at a lower cost than industry peers (owing to unwarranted state subsidies, or implicit or explicit guarantees on commercial debt), they can charge more competitive prices and undercut competition without necessarily offering products and services in the most productive manner. On the other hand, if SOEs must finance their operations at a higher cost than industry peers (e.g. if they are required to provide public services without adequate compensation, or distribute excessive dividends to support state budgetary needs), this can jeopardise their financial and commercial viability.

This report has a dual objective of (1) synthesising national practices with respect to the processes behind SOE financing decisions; and (2) taking stock of a range of financial transactions and conditions which might make the cost of operating SOEs materially different than for private competitors. The areas considered the most relevant to these objectives, and which were therefore included in the questionnaire on which this report is based, are organised in the following sections of the report.

Section 2. *Capital structure: Policy and implementation.* Capital structure efficiency concerns how well SOEs use the capital resources at their disposal to create value for their owners and shareholders. When a focus on SOEs' capital efficiency and value creation gives way to public policy concerns or state budgetary needs, SOEs are no longer operating on competitively neutral terms with private competitors. Such departures from competitive neutrality can occur notably through reductions in rate-of return requirements imposed on SOEs, but also through unwarranted capital outflows (e.g. SOE dividend pay-outs that are not justified by company performance) or excessive capital inflows (e.g. direct state subsidies that confer a competitive advantage on SOEs' commercial activities). The relevant subsections discuss these capital structure issues in detail as follows:

- *Determining an optimal capital structure* examines the extent to which the authorities have elaborated guiding principles for determining and maintaining an optimal capital structure. It also examines the respective roles and responsibilities of the state ownership function, SOE boards and SOE management in making decisions that affect SOEs' capital structure.
- *Establishing rate-of-return requirements* takes stock of existing rate-of-return requirements for SOEs and describes the extent to which SOEs are held accountable for their fulfilment.
- *Setting dividend levels* provides an overview of the main reported factors taken into account when determining annual dividend levels for SOEs, including any broad dividend guidelines developed by national authorities. It also describes national practices concerning the annual negotiation of dividend levels, and the respective roles of the ownership function, SOE boards and management in determining annual dividend levels.
- *Providing direct state support* gives an overview of the conditions and modalities for providing direct state support to SOEs, where such support is possible. It also identifies countries where direct state support is not provided to SOEs.

Section 3. *Sources and conditions of SOE financing.* Beyond the principles and transactions directly impacting SOE capitalisation, this section examines more specifically the terms and conditions surrounding equity and debt financing, how they compare with private competitors, and any mechanisms to neutralise SOEs' potential financial advantages.

- *Recapitalising SOEs* provides information on the processes and conditions regarding SOE recapitalisations from the public budget. It notably looks at whether public budget recapitalisations do occur; what form they generally take and the associated costs (including mechanisms in place to approximate market consistent equity costs); and, where relevant, the extent to which minority shareholders are able to participate in recapitalisation decisions and the resulting capital issues.
- *Financing through debt* synthesises the main sources and forms of debt financing for SOEs. It notably includes information on whether SOEs access their debt financing on the commercial marketplace and/or from the state treasury. When available, it also provides information on the main reported forms of debt financing, notably the extent to which SOEs rely respectively on

commercial loans, tradable bonds and supplier or trade credits for their debt financing needs.

– *Identifying the cost of debt financing*. This section summarises the terms and conditions surrounding SOE debt financing. It notably looks at the availability and conditions of state guarantees on SOE debt; whether there is reported evidence of preferential financing terms for SOEs on the commercial market; and whether the authorities have put in place mechanisms to neutralise any potential cost advantages for SOEs' debt financing.

Section 4. *Remaining challenges to competitive neutrality* summarises the report's main findings and identifies some key persisting challenges to ensuring competitively neutral financing conditions for SOEs.

The level of policy elaboration concerning SOE financing varies significantly across economies. In a few countries, the ownership function has developed in-depth guidance, for example explicit guidelines on determining and maintaining an optimal capital structure, which then guide subsequent decisions regarding rate-of-return and dividend expectations. In other countries, such overarching guidelines do not exist and financing decisions are more frequently made on an *ad hoc* basis. The present report seeks to provide information both on any established policy guidelines along the above categories, and on actual practices as reported by respondent countries.

National practices regarding SOE financing are by no means homogenous across all SOEs in a given country. Indeed, even against the backdrop of any established guidelines developed by the national authorities (which only exist in some countries), SOE financing decisions are often made on a case-by-case basis, with the state ownership function exercising varying degrees of involvement and oversight. Additionally, the financial governance practices of SOEs can vary significantly between those that operate on an entirely commercial basis, and those that (while of a primarily commercial nature) also fulfil public service obligations. For these and other reasons, synthesising national practices with respect to SOE financing can be a complex task. The questionnaire requested that respondents synthesise the 3-4 most commonly occurring financing models in their responses.

Finally, for the purpose of this report, an effort has been made to focus mostly on national practices toward fully incorporated SOEs of a largely commercial nature. SOEs whose primary purpose is to fulfil public service obligations or achieve sectoral policy objectives are generally not included. However, SOEs of a largely commercial nature that *also* fulfil public service obligations are entirely relevant for the purpose of the report. Indeed, in situations where SOEs have the dual objectives of competing on a commercial market and fulfilling public service obligations, any material differences in their financing conditions will effectively impact the competitive landscape shared with their private sector peers, thus becoming an issue of competitive neutrality.

2. Capital structure: Policy and implementation

Maintaining market consistent, or competitively neutral, financing costs can be particularly challenging for SOEs. Financing may be provided on preferential terms (directly by the state treasury, and/or by state-owned or commercial banks), or the state as an owner could impose rate-of-return and dividend requirements inconsistent with private sector practices. Capital structure policy is important because it concerns (i) how, and at what cost, SOEs finance their operations (i.e. the mix of debt and equity financing and whether it is obtained at market rates); and (ii) how SOEs use these capital resources to create value for their investors and owners (ultimately the broader public). While all companies face challenges in maintaining an optimal capital structure – among them achieving an appropriate balance between profit reinvestment and dividend distribution – SOEs may face additional constraints owing to their state ownership. Departures from competitive neutrality can notably occur when public policy and temporary state budgetary concerns become predominant factors in decisions relating to SOEs' capital structure. Avoiding such situations requires high standards of governance and a continued focus on capital efficiency and value creation, at all stages in the SOE's corporate life cycle.

Decisions impacting SOEs' capital structure take place in several phases, notably: (i) at the time of company establishment, based primarily on planned capital investment needs and the relative costs of debt and equity financing; and (ii) throughout the corporate life cycle, based on the interplay between company profits (or losses), the financial returns required by investors (i.e. dividend pay-outs and rate-of-return expectations) and/or decisions to infuse fresh funds.

In some countries, after SOE establishment, the state ownership function remains continually involved in discussions relating to the achievement of a financially optimal capital structure. In other countries, it is customary for SOE boards take the lead with operational capital structure decisions, and the state's involvement is implicit, embodied in its announced dividend expectations or rate-of-return targets. In all cases, one may assume that few SOE boards are able to make autonomous decisions about SOE capital structure without regard to the expectations of the state as owner and investor (whether communicated via regular consultations, broad guidelines, pre-established financial targets, or on an *ad-hoc* basis).

The first section below focuses on the respective roles and responsibilities of the state and SOE boards in determining SOEs' capital structure, including whether the authorities communicate broad guidelines on the subject. Beyond the level of such broad guidelines, a number of financial transactions and conditions that take place throughout the corporate life cycle have an impact on SOE capital structure, and ultimately on the establishment of competitively neutral financing conditions. These are discussed in detail in the remainder of the report as follows: the establishment of rate-of-return requirements; the annual dividend setting process; and the provision of direct state support to finance public service obligations or rescue failing companies.

Determining an optimal capital structure

It bears mentioning that not all respondent countries have recent experience with SOE establishment on which to base their descriptions of the respective roles and responsibilities of the state and SOE boards in identifying an optimal capital structure. Among the 13 countries that do report having recently established SOEs, the majority cite public service delivery as the driving factor behind their establishment, with a handful of new SOEs emerging in the utilities, transportation and financial sectors. In a few cases, the recent establishment of SOEs reportedly reflects the incorporation of state-owned statutory or quasi-corporations (Finland and Sweden). For further details on recent cases of SOE establishment (including state acquisition of ownership in private companies), see Annex at the end of this report.

Given this difference in recent national experiences, throughout this section it should be kept in mind that questionnaire respondents might be referring to different stages of the corporate life cycle when reporting on the respective roles of the state and SOE boards in capital structure decisions. For example, those reporting a significant board influence in capital structure decisions clearly do not have the SOE establishment phase in mind. They must logically refer to on-going processes which influence capital structure, such as the establishment of annual dividend targets. Conversely, some respondents have limited responses to the SOE establishment phase, many of whom report that SOE capital structure decisions are uniquely the purview of the state.

Comparing national practices is therefore not a simple task. An effort has been made to synthesise country practices into four categories according to the level and type of state involvement in capital structure decisions, according to established policy. However, in practice, the respective roles of the state and SOE boards may not be so clear cut, and may in some cases reflect differences of form rather than substance. As discussed elsewhere, given the fiscal implications of SOEs' capital needs and dividend yields, it is unlikely that the higher levels of government give no attention to this issue. Also, where respondents report that SOE boards of directors are relatively free to make their own decisions, it must be kept in mind that these directors need to consider the spectre of government intervention if their decisions deviate too far from what is politically expedient.

The ways in which capital structure decisions are made regarding SOEs vary among respondent countries, both in terms of (i) the division of responsibility and level of communication between SOE boards and the ownership function and (ii) the level of policy guidance elaborated by the authorities regarding how to determine an optimal capital structure. Most respondent countries report that capital structure decisions are primarily the purview of SOE boards and management, with the ownership function exercising varying degrees of oversight, ranging from limited government involvement, to the provision of clear and explicit guidelines for identifying an appropriate capital structure, to direct review and approval. Regarding the principles and processes behind capital structure decisions, respondent countries can be broadly divided into four groups (a synthesis is provided in Table 1):

1. *SOE boards have primary responsibility, no explicit governmental guidelines.* In a first group of countries, SOE boards and management have primary responsibility for capital structure decisions and the authorities do not communicate explicit guidelines or benchmarks for developing an optimal capital structure. In some of these countries, questionnaire responses indicate that the authorities are directly consulted only in cases of capital inadequacy where new equity issues are requested (Germany, Slovenia). In Lithuania, SOE board responsibility for capital structure decisions is enshrined in law[2].

2. *Capital structure decisions by SOE boards take into account explicit governmental guidelines.* In a second group of countries, SOE boards and management take the lead regarding capital structure decisions, but taking into account clear governmental guidance. In these countries, the authorities communicate explicit guidelines for developing an optimal capital structure, most often taking the form of an announced credit rating target, which is used as a benchmark for all subsequent decisions impacting capital structure (Australia, Ireland for large SOEs, the Netherlands, New Zealand, Sweden and Switzerland). In such cases, the maintenance of an investment grade credit rating acts as a mechanism to ensure efficient financial governance and discipline, in line with

competitive private sector practices. Box 1 provides a description of the policies and processes behind capital structure decisions for SOEs in Australia.

Within this group, the Swedish authorities in particular have elaborated a step-by-step process for determining the capital structure of SOEs, which takes into account the interdependence between capital efficiency, rate-of-return requirements and dividend pay-outs. As shown in Figure 1, capital structure decisions for existing SOEs in Sweden are structured around four meetings, each with clearly defined goals, dedicated respectively to (i) identifying the theoretical cost of capital; (ii) discussing a desired capital structure and the company's forecasted performance; (iii) based on this information, formulating relevant rate-of-return and dividend targets; and (iv) presenting a consolidated view of the capital structure to the board.

Figure 1. **Process for SOE capital structure decisions in Sweden**

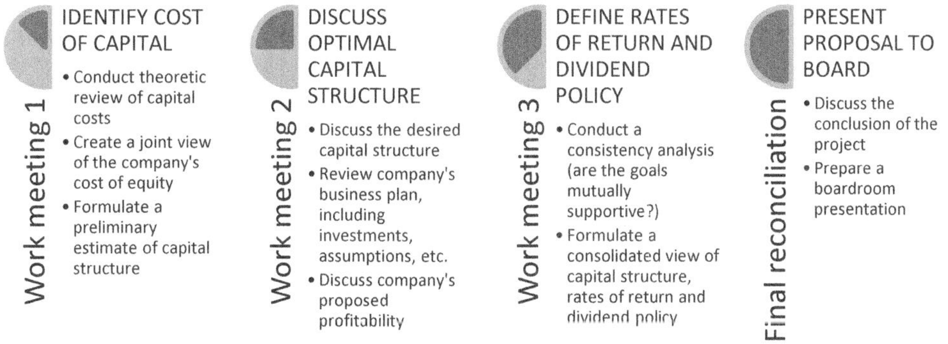

Source: Submission by Swedish authorities in response to OECD questionnaire.

Box 1. **Identifying an optimal capital structure for SOEs in Australia**

Australia's commercial SOEs are called Government Business Enterprises (GBEs). GBEs report to Shareholder Ministers and follow the Commonwealth Government Business Enterprise Governance and Oversight Guidelines (GBE Guidelines). The GBE Guidelines state "each GBE should target an optimal capital structure (the combination of financial liabilities and equity used to fund the assets of the GBE) that is agreed annually between the board and the Shareholder Minister(s) in the corporate plan consultation process."

A GBE's Board is responsible for development of capital structure as part of the annual corporate planning process. The Corporate Plan is submitted by Boards to Shareholder Minister/s each financial year and is the key planning document of the GBE.

The GBE Guidelines advise that an optimal capital structure is one that, in light of economic, industry and GBE specific factors, would provide for an investment grade credit rating, whilst at the same time imposing a discipline on the GBE to optimise efficiency. The target credit rating is BBB.

As part of developing a target optimal capital structure, consideration will be given to the forecast level of capital expenditure in the GBE's annual corporate plan, and appropriate options for funding capital expenditure (including via retained earnings or debt). Consideration will also be given to longer term objectives outlined in a GBE's annual corporate plan.

In providing for a GBE to expand its capital base through retained earnings, any proposed future capital expenditure should add shareholder value. That is, as a minimum, capital expenditure plans should meet a hurdle rate-of-return (weighted average cost of capital (WACC)) that is consistent with the GBE's principal financial target.

The capital structure of a GBE reflects the relevant risk of the entity, the environment it operates in and the economic conditions at the time. Capital structures are benchmarked against private sector entities to the extent possible.

Source: Submission by Australian authorities in response to OECD questionnaire.

3. *Capital structure decisions by SOE boards subject to approval at annual general meeting.* In a third group of countries, no explicit guidelines are in place but the authorities exercise influence over SOEs' capital structure decisions through their participation in the annual general meeting.

4. *State ownership function has primary responsibility for capital structure decisions.* In a fourth group of countries, all capital structure decisions are subject to direct approval by the state ownership function. In these

countries, SOE boards and management make proposals regarding capital structure, which are then reviewed by the relevant body(ies) (i.e. state ownership entity, treasury, ministry of finance and/or shareholding ministries). Within this group, the nuance should be added that in two countries government approval procedures are supplemented with explicit financial targets or guidelines:

- In the case of Estonia, explicit annual capital structure targets are agreed between the state ownership function and SOE boards, based on financial performance forecasts, investment needs and proposed dividend levels.
- In Canada, the Financial Risk Management Guidelines for Crown Corporations set out the Ministry of Finance's expectations regarding the financial risk management practices of SOEs, which then influences capital structure decisions.

Table 1. **Process for capital structure decisions**

SOE boards have primary responsibility, no explicit governmental guidelines	**Germany:** The initial capital structure of SOEs is decided upon by the responsible ministry at the time of SOE establishment, after which legal stipulations make capital structure decisions the sole responsibility of SOE management boards. **Lithuania:** By law, boards and/or CEOs hold the responsibility to decide upon capital structure, and the government can only communicate its expectations in the form of a recommendation. Ownership Guidelines do allow for the government to establish capital structure expectations for SOEs, but in practice this has not been done. The Commercial Company Code requires all joint stock companies to allocate 8% of yearly net profit to a reserve capital until it reaches one third of the share capital. This reserve capital can only be used to finance losses. This provision is voluntary for limited liability companies. **Slovenia:** SOE management boards determine capital structure. In case of significant planned changes to capital structure, management boards require consent of supervisory board. Only in cases of capital inadequacy, boards may propose to shareholding ministries a capital increase.
Capital structure decisions by SOE boards take into account explicit governmental guidelines	**Australia:** Capital structure is agreed annually between Government Business Enterprise boards and shareholder minister(s) as part of the annual corporate planning process, taking into account credit rating target of BBB outlined in the Government Business Enterprise Guidelines. **Ireland:** SOE boards prepare five year business plans including proposed capital structure, as stipulated by the Code of Practice for Governance of State Bodies. Business plans are sent to ministerial shareholders for their feedback. While there are no written policies regarding the calculation of an optimal capital structure for all SOEs, in practice large SOEs are expected to put in place an appropriate capital structure (with specific targets developed for individual SOEs).

	Netherlands: SOE management decides on capital structure, taking into account Ministry of Finance's general guidelines that all SOEs should put in place a capital structure to maintain investment grade credit ratings. Share issuance requires shareholder approval, while contracting debt does not. **New Zealand:** SOE boards determine optimum capital structure, taking into account the Crown Ownership Monitoring Unit's (COMU) announced credit rating target. COMU is consulted in cases of significant planned changes to capital structure (no surprises policy). **Sweden:** Capital structure decisions are made at the annual general meeting taking into account explicit guidelines of the Ministry of Finance's Ownership Unit. Prior consultations are held between the MoF Ownership Unit and SOE boards. **Switzerland:** SOE boards lead decision-making process, taking into account the Federal Council's explicit annual guidelines on debt and dividend levels for individual SOEs. Parliament Act is necessary for SOE recapitalisations.
Capital structure decisions by SOE boards subject to approval at annual general meeting	**Czech Republic:** SOE boards and management present proposed capital structure at the annual general meeting. **Finland:** SOE boards and management decide independently on type and amount of external financing and make proposal at the annual general meeting regarding dividend levels. Ownership Steering Department in the Prime Minister's Office provides feedback via informal discussion with boards prior to AGM. **Poland:** SOE management boards formulate capital structure proposals which are reviewed by supervisory boards and subject to approval at the annual general meeting. Ministry of Treasury participates in its capacity as company shareholder. **United Kingdom:** Practices vary depending on type of SOE, but in general the state's involvement in capital structure decisions ranges from strong oversight to full control (therefore practices for some SOEs would fall into the fourth category)[3]. In most cases, the role of SOE boards is to make proposals or requests to the state ownership function concerning changes to the capital structure. There is no overall guiding principle for determining SOEs' optimal capital structure, but in practice many SOEs use credit rating targets. Practices according to the three main types of SOE can be summarised as follows. (1) In the case of minority-owned SOEs (e.g. the nuclear company Urenco which is one-third owned by the U.K. government), boards take the lead on operational capital structure decisions, with the state exercising oversight via the appointment of non-executive directors. Any major decisions impacting capital structure or dividend pay-out are discussed at Shareholder Forums, in which the state participates in its capacity as shareholder. (2) Wholly-owned government businesses can be fully funded by state equity; changes to capital structure require approval of the Secretary of State for the Government Department and the treasury. (3) For wholly-owned SOEs that can receive funding in the commercial marketplace, the source and amount of loans is agreed upon in advance and documented via a Trading Fund Order and Treasury Minute.

State ownership function has primary responsibility for capital structure decisions	**Canada:** SOE boards are required to submit an annual corporate plan and budget (which include proposed capital structure) to the Governor in Council and the Treasury Board for their approval. The corporate plans and budgets are developed by SOE management, approved by SOE boards and then submitted to the responsible minister. The final decision on capital structure is the responsibility of the Ministers of the Treasury Board upon recommendation of the responsible minister and in consultation with the Treasury Board Secretariat and the Department of Finance. A handful of SOEs is exempted from the requirement to submit annual corporate plans and budgets to the Governor in Council, in order to shield them from actual or perceived political interference in the fulfilment of their mandates. **Chile:** SOE boards propose optimum capital structure to Public Enterprise Committee, who submits technical recommendation to Ministry of Finance for review and approval. Capital injections require legal approval via the Budget Law. **Estonia:** SOE management boards prepare annual reports, including five-year financial forecasts, projected investment needs, proposed dividend levels and debt financing ability. On the basis of these reports, shareholding ministry(ies) and ministry of finance determine capital structure and return on equity targets, which are communicated to SOEs via the annual state shareholdings report. Consideration is given to optimising SOEs' return on equity, notably through maintaining a reasonable amount of debt leverage. **Hungary:** Two processes possible: (1) SOE boards and management propose capital structure to shareholding ministries who make final approval or (2) shareholding ministries request information from SOE boards and on that basis determine the capital structure. **Israel:** SOE boards decide upon capital structure, under the monitoring and supervision of the Government Companies Authority and within the framework imposed by the SOE's establishment legislation. A number of decisions made by SOE boards are explicitly subject to subsequent government approval, as stipulated in the Government Companies Law. They include, among others: bond issuance and changes in share capital, as well as any transactions wherein an SOE grants a right or assumes an obligation that could, directly or indirectly, restrict the government in its status as shareholder or in the exercise of its governmental functions. Such governmental functions as explicitly referenced in the Government Companies Law include: the implementation of structural changes and privatisation; the promotion of competition; and the regulation of the sector in which the SOE operates [Art. 11(a) of the Government Companies Law]. **Italy:** Initial equity levels are determined by the legislation establishing the SOE. All decisions related to equity levels are the unique responsibility of the Italian Ministry of Economy and Finance. SOE boards and management can only make decisions regarding debt levels. **Japan:** For SOEs included in the reporting sample, boards and management make decisions regarding capital structure, which are then submitted to the government for approval. For airport companies, new equity issues require approval from SOE board and Minister of Land, Infrastructure, Transport and Tourism. For both airport and expressway companies, SOE establishment legislation stipulates that a minimum amount of voting shares must be held by the government (100% for most airport companies, at least 1/3 for expressway companies).

	Korea: The government does not independently establish the capital structure of SOEs; boards are involved in decisions relating to corporate bond issuance and, in some cases, new equity issuance. In some cases, the establishment legislation of certain SOEs stipulates maximum debt-to-equity ratios and requires the approval of responsible ministries in order to pursue certain changes to the capital structure. For example, the establishment legislation of Korea Land and Housing Corporation stipulates that in case of corporate bond issuance, the value of bonds must not exceed double the company's capital and reserves, and all bond issuance requires prior approval of the Minister of Land, Infrastructure and Transportation. In some cases (e.g. Korea District Heating Corporation) SOE boards are permitted to raise new equity capital, under the condition of maintaining state majority ownership. While no capital structure guidelines are in place for SOEs, they are required to elaborate medium- and long-term financial management plans to manage their debt-to-equity ratio. **Norway:** The Ministry of Trade and Industry (hereinafter "the ownership Ministry") is responsible for the execution of the state's ownership in several commercial companies. According to the ownership policy established by parliament, the ownership Ministry is expected to contribute to an appropriate capital structure which enables those companies to achieve a favourable industrial development and efficient operations. In practice, the ownership Ministry generally requests that SOE boards provide an assessment of the company's capital structure prior to carrying out its own assessment and implementing measures to achieve an appropriate capitalisation. This process generally involves close dialogue between the ownership Ministry, SOE boards and management, and in cases of capital structure adjustments, the Ministry of Finance.

Source: Submissions by national authorities in response to OECD questionnaire.

Establishing rate-of-return requirements

Rates of return relate to how efficiently SOEs use the capital resources at their disposal to create value through their commercial activities. When wholly commercial SOEs are required to achieve rates of return consistent with private sector actors, this promotes a more efficient allocation of capital resources in the broader economy, by ensuring that capital is channelled to the most productive activities. However, establishing appropriate rates of return can be challenging when SOEs are engaged in both commercial and non-commercial activities, especially if those activities are not structurally separated. Requiring an SOE to deliver public services at below-market cost while also maintaining commercial returns imposes an undue burden that is not consistent with competitive neutrality. OECD recommendations, including the SOE Guidelines, imply that the cost of non-commercial priorities for SOEs should be covered through targeted subsidies, with commercial rate-of-return requirements only applied to SOEs' commercial activities. However, in practice in cases where structural separation has not been established between commercial and non-commercial activities, the authorities do not infrequently compensate the companies by imposing a lower rate-of-return on an SOE's entire portfolio of activities (one respondent conceding that this is the case is Lithuania).

In most of the countries where the authorities have elaborated some form of capital structure guideline, the same authorities also communicate explicit rate-of-return requirements. National practices regarding rate-of-return targets and monitoring can be broadly summarised as follows (for further details, see Table 2):

1. *Rate-of-return targets established by ownership function or SOE boards.* In about three quarters of reporting countries, explicit rate-of-return targets for SOEs are elaborated either directly by the authorities, or by SOE boards in close consultation with the authorities. In some of these cases, the ownership function elaborates guidelines that are broad enough to be applicable to the entire SOE sector, while in other cases it sets annual targets for individual SOEs, taking into account sector-relevant benchmarks. Some specific practices merit elaboration:

    - In three countries, SOE rate-of-return targets are established primarily by SOE boards, with the ownership function providing feedback on targets through the corporate planning process (Canada, Finland and Slovenia). In Finland, this feedback takes the form of frequent dialogue between SOE boards and the ownership entity. In Slovenia, when SOEs do not achieve the financial targets expressed in their annual plans, board members can be dismissed.

    - In four countries, the ownership function and SOE boards communicate specific details on the calculation used for identifying the cost of capital when calculating rates of return (this applies to Estonia, Lithuania, New Zealand, Norway and Sweden). Box 2 provides an example from Estonia on calculating rate-of-return targets based on the Capital Asset Pricing Model.

    - In most of the cases where explicit rate-of-return guidelines exist, these are usually discussed during the annual corporate planning process. SOEs are then expected to take into account agreed targets in the elaboration of the annual business plan or statement of corporate intent. The achievement of the targets can then be used as a basis for measuring and monitoring SOE performance.

2. *No rate-of-return targets.* In a minority of countries, the authorities do not establish explicit rate-of-return requirements for the SOE sector. However, within this group, the authorities in two countries do report that they (being the regulators) have developed return requirements for SOEs in regulated industries (Ireland, Israel).

Box 2. **Calculating rate-of-return targets for SOEs: An example from Estonia**

In Estonia, return-on-equity (ROE) targets are established by the ministry of finance and communicated via the annual state shareholdings report. ROE is calculated based on a modified Capital Asset Pricing Model as follows:

$$R_e = R_f + B_e(R_m - R_f) + R_s$$

Where:

R_e	=	expected ROE i.e. cost of equity,
R_f	=	risk-free interest rate,
β_e	=	leveraged beta,
R_m-R_f	=	market risk premium (market interest rate minus the risk-free interest rate),
R_s	=	risk premium on enterprise size.

The risk-free interest rate applied is calculated as an average of the ten-year government bond rates of EU countries with the same country credit rating as Estonia. (Estonia has not issued government bonds on which to base the risk-free interest rate). In cases where no EU country has the same credit rating as Estonia, an average of the countries whose rating is in range of plus or minus one notch of Estonia's country credit rating is used.

The leveraged beta applied is equal to a sector-specific beta multiplied by the SOE's leverage (debt-to-equity ratio) projected in its capital structure forecasts. The sector-specific beta is taken from an online database of sectoral betas (http://people.stern.nyu.edu/adamodar/New_Home_Page/datafile/Betas.html).

The market risk premium used is 5%, as recommended by the country's competition authority based on what is considered good practice.

The premium on enterprise size is calculated based on a measure of individual SOE performance, taking into account: (1) diversification of customer portfolio; (2) diversification of product portfolio; (3) management quality; (4) revenue stability; and (5) financial ability. A higher performance indicator will lead to a lower risk premium.

Source: Submission by Estonian authorities in response to OECD questionnaire.

Table 2. **Establishing rate-of-return targets for SOEs**

Countries where rate-of-return targets are established for SOEs (either by the ownership function or via proposition of SOE boards)	**Australia:** Government Business Enterprise Guidelines stipulate that SOEs (GBEs in the national nomenclature) must earn a commercial rate-of-return at least sufficient to justify long term retention of assets in the business and to pay commercial dividends from those returns. Shareholder Ministers and Government Business Enterprise boards agree annually on financial targets based on these guidelines. **Canada:** Financial targets are developed by SOEs and reviewed by the government through the annual corporate plan process. In case of non-fulfilment of financial targets, the government can influence the company's directions through the corporate plan process or by issuing a targeted directive. **Chile:** Public Enterprises Committee establishes annual ROR targets for companies in its portfolio. **Estonia:** Return on equity targets are established in the annual state shareholdings report. The report includes details for calculating the cost of capital, using the Capital Asset Pricing Model. **Finland:** Rate-of-return targets are not established by the authorities, but the Ownership Steering Department in the Prime Minister's Office can provide feedback on the targets set by SOE boards and management, via regular dialogue with them. Targets are typically included, among other performance indicators, in the incentive plans for SOE management. **Hungary:** Hungarian National Asset Management Inc. communicates rate-of-return targets to individual SOEs in its portfolio through annual planning principles, which are used by companies in the elaboration of their business plans. **Korea:** The authorities do not establish explicit rate-of-return requirements, but SOE boards define financial targets through an in-company decision-making process. **Lithuania:** Ministerial resolution stipulates that SOEs achieve a rate-of-return on equity of 5% for the period 2013-2015, and comparable rates as industry peers as of 2016. SOEs' cost of capital is calculated based on the Capital Asset Pricing Model. Rate-of-return targets apply to SOEs' entire portfolio of activities, including non-commercial. **New Zealand:** Government ownership guidelines communicate the expectation that SOEs achieve a total shareholder return exceeding their cost of capital over a five year period, and that SOEs publish performance data on ten financial performance targets established in the annual Statement of Corporate Intent. Individual SOEs are expected to communicate on an annual basis their cost of capital and underpinning calculations to the Crown Ownership Monitoring Unit. **Netherlands:** 2007 ownership policy guidelines communicate a return on equity expectation for all SOEs of 8%[4].

	Norway: According to the state's Regulations for Financial Management in the Government Administration, rate-of-return targets must be established for companies in which the state is a shareholder. The methodology for establishing rate-of-return targets is based on the Capital Asset Pricing Model. The targets are conveyed to SOE boards and management and are not publicly available. In practice, SOE rate-of-return targets serve as a reference over time, rather than as an explicit requirement. However, the achievement of targets is closely monitored and plays a significant role in board evaluations. Failing to meet the targets over time would generally necessitate closer assessment and possibly changes in the ownership structure and/or capital structure of the concerned SOE. **Slovenia:** Explicit rate-of-return targets are not defined by the authorities, but supervisory boards of individual SOEs propose return on equity targets in the yearly plan. **Sweden:** The Ministry of Finance Ownership Unit defines explicit rate-of-return requirements via the ownership policy, and provides detailed calculation guidelines, based on the Capital Asset Pricing Model. **Switzerland:** The Federal Council defines rate-of-return and earnings targets for most companies in its portfolio, communicated via the four-yearly strategic objectives for individual SOEs. SOEs report annually on the achievement of these targets. **United Kingdom:** The Shareholding Department regularly establishes rate-of-return targets for individual SOEs, often in the form of a target Return on Average Capital Employed (ROACE). Targets are agreed annually between the Shareholder Executive and the SOE. Accountability mechanisms are strong and can include yearly reporting to parliament and the public, and linking executive bonuses to the achievement of targets.
Countries with no rate-of-return targets	In the following five countries, no reported rate-of-return targets exist for the SOE sector: **Czech Republic, Germany, Ireland, Israel, Italy, Japan** and **Poland**[5].

Source: Submissions by national authorities in response to OECD questionnaire.

Setting dividend levels

How the government makes decisions or communicates expectations regarding SOE dividend levels varies greatly across countries. But given that SOE dividends are a source of revenue for the fiscal budget, there is little doubt that the government will indeed make its expectations heard at some stage in the process. In some countries, the state's dividend expectations are communicated to SOE boards each year on a case-by-case basis. In other countries, annual dividend negotiations take place against the backdrop of established guidelines and/or explicit targets elaborated by the state ownership function. In three countries, an interesting model exists whereby the state's dividend expectations, communicated via established guidelines, are explicitly linked to the achievement of an optimal capital structure as measured by the maintenance of a target credit rating (See Box 4 for an example from Australia). To summarise, respondent countries can roughly be divided into four groups according to the level of policy elaboration for determining annual SOE dividend pay-outs (for further details, see Table 3):

1. *No dividend guidelines or targets.* In a first group of countries, no explicit dividend guidelines or targets are in place. Annual dividend levels are negotiated annually between SOE boards and owners at the annual general meeting or in the framework of the annual corporate plan consultation process (Chile, Czech Republic, Estonia, Finland, Germany, Hungary, Italy, Japan and Korea).

2. *Broad guidelines.* In a second, smaller group of countries, the authorities elaborate broad guidelines applicable to the entire SOE sector concerning what factors should be taken into account in setting dividend levels (Israel, Korea and Poland). (See Box 3 for a description of dividend guidelines in Poland). In Canada and the United Kingdom, there is no overall dividend policy for the aggregate SOE portfolio, but dividend frameworks for individual SOEs are elaborated via consultations between SOE boards and the state shareholder.

3. *Explicit percentage of net income.* In a third group of countries, dividend expectation levels are generally calculated as a pre-defined target percentage of net income (Ireland, Lithuania, Norway, Slovenia and Switzerland).

4. *Linked to optimal capital structure.* In a fourth, smaller group of countries, the authorities communicate broad expectations regarding dividend levels, linking annual pay-out ratios to the achievement of an optimal capital structure. In these cases, the authorities communicate a target credit rating by which to measure the optimal capital structure, and this acts as an overarching guiding principle for annual dividend pay-out levels. This applies to Australia, New Zealand, the Netherlands and Sweden[6]. In the case of the Netherlands, all SOEs are expected to maintain an investment grade credit rating, and this guides all decisions related to SOEs' capital structure. Box 4 provides an excerpt of the Australian state ownership entity's guidelines regarding dividend levels and capital structure.

Box 3. Guiding principles for profit distribution of majority- and wholly-owned SOEs in Poland

The decision regarding dividend levels of SOEs in Poland lies with SOE boards. However, each year, the Minister of Treasury elaborates guidelines regarding the reporting standards and "profit sharing" (including dividends) of companies that are wholly- or majority-owned by the Treasury. These guidelines take the form of general provisions designed to contribute to the sound management of resources (including dividends), but they do not indicate the level of dividends or their specific amounts. The below is an unofficial translation of an excerpt of those guidelines.

In terms of the rules of collecting dividends arising from the achieved economic result of the company, the Ministry of Treasury will be guided by the following principles:

1. **Applying an individual approach to each individual company's situation, the decision-making process will primarily take into account:**
   a) the need to cover any remaining losses from previous years,
   b) investment plans resulting from the long-term strategy adopted by the Supervisory Board or other detailed documents, such as development plan, restructuring schedule, project's business plan etc.,
   c) progress of the privatisation process; as a rule, increased dividend should be collected in companies in which these processes are advanced,
   d) the company's indebtedness.

2. **The General Meeting/Meeting of Shareholders waives the right to collect dividend if:**
   a) total losses from previous years recognised in the company's balance sheet are higher than the net profit for the financial year,
   b) the Treasury, in the given year, provides the company with financial assistance (subsidies), guarantees its loans or redeems its debts.

3. **The General Meeting/Meeting of Shareholders may waive the right to collect dividends in whole or in part in justified cases**, in particular when the Company's authorities motion the allocation of the entire or part of the net profit for supplementary

capital or reserve capital (specifically designated for development purposes - increase of non-financial fixed assets) with indication of specific projects and tasks resulting from the development strategy adopted by the Supervisory Board and due to take place in this financial year according to this strategy.

4. **Upon the request of the company and verification of its validity, a decision on collection of the dividend is made. The dividend shall be determined taking into account parameters such as:**

   a) Return on equity, calculated for net profit but also for the achieved operating profit comparing the achieved return of the enterprise to an average in the supervised industry.

   b) Profitability ratio calculated in relation to operating profit. Reference to operating profit will allow a more precise determination of the result achieved by the company on its core business and exclusion of changes resulting from casual events.

   c) ROA, ROE indicators (return on assets and equity) which when compared to bank interest rates on borrowed funds should show evidence of effective management in the company.

   d) Liquidity ratios which, if they show values far exceeding the values deemed optimum by the industry (i.e. by auditors reviewing financial statements), should result in revision of the reasons for accumulation of excessive funds in the company.

Source: Submission by Polish authorities in response to OECD questionnaire.

Box 4. **Linking dividends to optimal capital structure in Australia**

(Excerpt from the Commonwealth Government Business Enterprise Governance and Oversight Guidelines)

4.1 Each GBE should target an optimal capital structure (the combination of financial liabilities and equity used to fund the assets of the GBE) that is agreed annually between the board and the Shareholder Minister(s) in the corporate plan consultation process.

a) An optimal capital structure is one that, in light of economic, industry and GBE specific factors, would provide for an investment grade credit rating, whilst at the same time imposing a discipline on the GBE to optimise efficiency. The target credit rating is BBB.

b) As part of developing a target optimal capital structure, consideration will be given to the forecast level of capital expenditure in the GBE's annual corporate plan, and appropriate options for funding capital expenditure (including via retained earnings or debt). Consideration will also be given to longer term objectives outlined in a GBE's annual corporate plan.

c) In providing for a GBE to expand its capital base through retained earnings, any proposed future capital expenditure should add shareholder value. That is, as a minimum, capital expenditure plans should meet a hurdle rate-of-return that is consistent with the GBE's principal financial target (Refer 1.8 and 4.7 'Financial Targets for GBEs').

4.2 A GBE's level of estimated dividends (and forecast pay-out ratio) is to be agreed annually between the directors and the Shareholder Minister(s) through the corporate plan consultation process and should have regard to the maintenance of, or progress toward, its optimal capital structure.

a) The level of estimated dividends shall be driven by the desired capital structure, the profitability of the enterprise, and the level of agreed future capital expenditure.

b) The proposed dividend pay-out ratio and estimated dividend payment should be included in the corporate plan for each year covered by the plan.

c) The agreed dividend pay-out ratio should take account of the Government's preference for dividends over capital gains.

d) Profits generated by subsidiaries are to be taken into account in agreeing the level of estimated dividends and forecast pay-out ratio.

4.3 Dividends should be paid in two instalments: an interim dividend and a final dividend.

a) Interim dividends are paid by 30 April and final dividends by 31 October.

b) The Shareholder Minister(s) may agree on variations to those dates, after consultation with the board of the GBE.

4.4 Interim and final dividends to be paid should be agreed between the board and the Shareholder Minister(s), as soon as possible after the half yearly progress reports for the periods ending December and June have been received by the Shareholder Minister(s).

4.5 The capital structure of a GBE is to be reviewed where the application of dividend policy has not led to, or is unlikely to lead to, an optimal capital structure within a reasonable period of time.

4.6. Dividend policy for partly owned GBEs should have regard to the above principles, the extent of Commonwealth ownership and the views of other shareholders.

Source: Excerpt from the Australian Government Department of Finance and Deregulation (2011), "Commonwealth Government Business Enterprise Governance and Oversight Guidelines",

http://www.finance.gov.au/publications/governance-arrangements/.

Table 3. **Dividend policies and practices**

No dividend guidelines or targets	**Chile:** There is no fixed dividend policy in place and dividend levels are not decided on the basis of maintaining a specific capital structure. In practice, SOE boards propose an annual dividend policy either directly to the Ministry of Finance or to the SEP (for companies in its portfolio) at the annual shareholders meeting. Annual dividend levels are decided taking into account SOEs' financial performance and future capital needs. For companies under the portfolio of the SEP, in practice SOEs are generally expected to distribute 100% of net income to the state in the form of dividends. **Czech Republic:** The authorities do not elaborate dividend guidelines. No information was provided on the general dividend setting process or the frequency of extraordinary dividends. However, an example was provided of a case where state budgetary needs influenced dividend levels. In this case, the authorities enacted a governmental decree calling for the transfer of the state-owned electricity company CEZ's ordinary dividends to finance the deficit of the Czech state pension system. **Estonia:** There is no guiding principle regarding dividend levels. Dividends are negotiated on the company level and determined according to the SOE's capital structure, cash flows, future investment needs and ability to use debt financing. Dividend planning occurs in parallel with the four-year state budget planning process. The process is as follows: (i) SOEs present five-year financial forecasts (including proposed dividend levels) to the shareholding ministry(ies) and ministry of finance for their approval; (ii) each year, SOEs propose dividend levels to the relevant shareholding ministry, then to the ministry of finance for review and approval; and (iii) final dividend levels are proposed to the Government for its approval. If shareholding ministry determines that the agreed dividend targets cannot be met (e.g. due to lower company performance), they must present a revised dividend proposal to the ministry of finance prior to voting in the shareholders meeting. The Government makes the final decision on how the shareholding ministry should vote at the shareholders' meeting, after receiving the new dividend proposal and opinion from the ministry of finance. Several extraordinary dividend pay-outs occurred in 2009, mainly due to higher-than-expected financial performance and/or an improved possibility to finance operations with debt. The increased pay-outs also helped to make the concerned SOEs' capital structure more efficient by improving their return on equity. **Finland:** SOE boards propose annual dividend levels at the annual general meeting following informal discussions with the Ownership Steering Department in the Prime Minister's Office. **Germany**: The central government holds ownership in only a handful of SOEs that pay a dividend. For those that are partially-owned, the government does not have a significant influence on dividend policy. For those that are wholly-owned, dividend levels are based exclusively on the net profit of the SOE and are negotiated annually at the AGM following the proposal of the management board. **Hungary**: There is no guiding principle regarding dividend levels. Dividends are determined on the individual company level based on profitability and future capital needs. There have been no instances of extraordinary dividend pay-outs.

	Italy: There is no overall guiding principle regarding dividend levels; dividends are negotiated annually between the SOE and the Ministry of Finance and are determined based on state budgetary needs and SOE profitability. **Japan:** There is no overall guiding principle regarding SOEs' dividend levels and the authorities are not involved in decisions relating to dividend pay-outs. SOEs which distribute dividends determine levels based on annual profitability. There have been no instances of extraordinary dividend pay-outs to report.
Broad guidelines	**Canada:** There is no overall guiding principle regarding SOE dividend levels for the entire SOE portfolio. Dividend policies are determined at the level of individual SOEs, based on their unique capital requirements and planned expenditures. In practice, dividend policies are developed by SOE boards, often in consultation with government bodies such as the Department of Finance and the Treasury Board Secretariat. Against this backdrop, annual dividend levels are proposed by SOE management in the corporate plan for approval by the responsible minister and the Treasury Board Ministers. The government can by law prescribe, waive or change the level of dividend pay-out by SOEs. In practice, extraordinary dividends are rare, but have occurred in cases of excess capital, usually through decision of the board, but in some cases resulting from a government decision. **Israel:** The Government Companies Authority communicates dividend guidelines to SOEs via two circulars on the subject. Extraordinary dividends do occur in cases of state budgetary needs. The government circulars outline the government policy regarding dividend rates and also mention factors to be considered when determining whether extraordinary dividends are necessary. In addition, the general companies law, which applies to SOEs, stipulates that companies can pay dividends given that they will not prevent the company from paying its existing and expected liabilities when they come due. **Korea:** The authorities have elaborated guiding principles and procedures for determining dividend levels, which stipulate that SOE dividends should take into account, among others (i) company financial performance and situation, including capital reserve level, debt/equity ratio, past dividend pay-outs and future investment needs; (ii) the financial needs of the government; and (iii) the pay-out ratios of private sector peers. Additionally, a Presidential Decree stipulates that dividend pay-out levels should also take into account whether SOEs receive state support and other matters deemed relevant by the Ministry of Strategy and Finance. Based on a process set forth by law, annual dividend levels are negotiated between SOE boards and the government, based on materials submitted by boards. There have been no reported instances of extraordinary dividend pay-outs. **Poland:** The Ministry of Treasury formulates annual guidelines for allocating the profits of wholly- and majority-owned SOEs. They take the form of general principles and stipulate, inter alia, that the calculation of SOE dividend levels should take into account individual companies' financial performance, future investment plans and stage in the privatisation process (if relevant). Annual dividend levels are determined at the annual general meeting. The guidelines also stipulate that company owners waive the right to collect a dividend if the state treasury provided the company, during the year in question, with subsidies, loan guarantees or payment of its debts. There have been recent examples of extraordinary dividend pay-outs, resulting from a decision by shareholders based on the excess capital and strong financial position of the concerned SOEs.

	United Kingdom: There is no overall guiding principle regarding dividend levels for the entire SOE portfolio. However, individual SOEs are often subject to broad dividend guidelines or specific targets, as in the following examples. For Green Investment Bank, dividend levels are grounded in an overall aim to reinvest, rather than distribute, profits. Ordnance Survey's dividend targets are based on company profitability. Royal Mint has an annual fixed dividend target of £4 mn. Met Office is required to pay an annual dividend at least equal to the required rate-of-return on average capital employed. The UK Hydrographic Office must at minimum distribute, in the form of dividend or interest payments, an amount at least equal to the capital cost faced by the relevant shareholding department. In practice, for SOEs that are not subject to an overall dividend guideline, pay-out levels are based primarily on company profitability, as well as shareholding department requirements, investment needs and cash reserve requirements. The only reported cases of extraordinary dividends occurred in cases of excess reserves.
Explicit percentage of net income	**Ireland**: There has been a general dividend expectation of 30% of net income, applicable to commercial SOEs regardless of sector. In most cases, this has not been formalised, although some individual SOEs do receive a letter of expectation from the relevant shareholding ministry explicitly outlining its dividend expectations. In practice, the New Economy and Recovery Authority (NewERA) is currently seeking to refine the dividend expectation setting process for its portfolio of SOEs. In this context, many SOEs will receive an annual letter of expectation from the relevant shareholding ministry, which is elaborated in consultation with the ownership function, and wherein the dividend expectations take into account individual SOEs' capital expenditure needs, as well as the goals of increasing shareholder value and achieving adequate credit ratings. Beyond these general elements, actual dividend levels can reportedly also be influenced by state budgetary needs as well as public policy objectives such as the development of the domestic economy. Extraordinary dividends have occurred in the past. **Lithuania:** The authorities communicate explicit dividend expectations to SOEs as follows: limited liability SOEs are required to pay dividends of at least 7% of equity but not exceeding 80% of company profits; statutory corporations are required to distribute 50% of annual profits in the form of dividends. Reductions in annual dividend pay-outs can be accorded by the Government of Lithuania at the request of the relevant shareholding ministry, for the implementation of strategic projects. Extraordinary dividends do occur, for example state-owned electricity companies paid out extraordinary dividends in 2012 owing to several years of accumulated profits and no dividend pay-out. **Netherlands:** The authorities have a general dividend expectation of 40% of net income, enshrined in the government's ownership policy. In practice, dividend levels are negotiated annually between SOEs boards and the Ministry of Finance, taking into account the pay-out ratios of comparable firms, the SOE's future investment needs and the achievement of the target credit rating. Extraordinary dividends have been paid out notably by two SOEs due to excess capital. **Norway:** The ownership Ministry communicates long term dividend expectations in writing to SOE boards, generally expressed as a percentage of income after minority interests. The expectations take into consideration a number of factors relating to: the company's actual and projected performance; industry-specific considerations; as well as additional factors such as the state's preference for stable or increasing dividend levels. In addition to these long term expectations (generally three to five years), the ownership Ministry establishes annual dividend expectations which are

	communicated orally to SOE boards before the boards submit their proposal to the annual general meeting. In practice, actual dividend levels are decided upon at the annual general meeting based on the board's proposal. The state as a shareholder can express its dividend expectations at the annual general meeting and explain the factors on which those expectations are based. However, for companies incorporated under the Limited Liabilities Companies Act/Public Limited Companies Act, the general meeting cannot decide to distribute a higher dividend than that proposed or approved by the board. There have been instances of extraordinary dividends, e.g. recently by the wholly state-owned construction company Mesta AS, owing to excess capitalisation. **Slovenia**: General dividend policy provides for a yearly pay-out of least one third of SOEs' net profit. This dividend policy was in the past communicated via a written document, and has since become common practice. Extraordinary dividends are rare but have in recent cases been used to cover temporary budgetary needs. **Switzerland:** The Federal Council communicates its dividend expectations to individual SOEs in its portfolio through the annual strategic objectives. These dividend expectations often take the form of a given percentage of net income or free cash flow, and are based on each SOE's expected profitability and future investment needs. If dividend levels need to be lowered due to lower-than-expected SOE performance, annual consultations occur between the Federal Council and the concerned SOE. There have been cases of extraordinary dividend pay-outs by SOEs, due to excess capital and strong financial performance; Swisscom is an example of this.
Linked to optimal capital structure	**Australia:** Annual dividend pay-out rates are agreed upon annually between boards of Government Business Enterprises and the shareholder minister(s) through the corporate plan consultation process. Explicit guidance is provided in the Government Business Enterprise Guidelines, which stipulate that dividend levels should be established with a view to achieving an optimal capital structure, taking into account company profitability and future capital expenditure needs. An optimal capital structure is defined as one that provides for an investment grade credit rating while optimising company efficiency (with a target of BBB). **New Zealand:** SOE boards set and publish their own dividend policies, taking into account the stated expectations of the Crown Ownership Monitoring Unit (COMU) (enshrined in its owner's expectations manual), which include optimal capital structure based on a target credit rating. Exact target dividend levels are discussed during the annual meeting between SOE boards and COMU and published in the Statement of Corporate Intent (SCI). **Sweden:** Individual SOE boards set their target dividend levels based on the objective of maintaining an optimum capital structure, following explicit governmental guidelines. The process is as follows: (1) SOEs determine their cost of capital based on the Capital Asset Pricing Model; (2) based on this, a capital structure is established and a profitability target set; (3) based on these parameters, a dividend policy is set.

Source: Submissions by national authorities in response to OECD questionnaire.

Beyond any established dividend guidelines in practice dividend levels are of course pragmatically influenced by SOEs' performance, their ability to access external financing for future capital needs, and in some cases, state budgetary needs. Although only a small group of countries reports that state budgetary needs influence yearly dividend levels (the Czech Republic, Ireland, Israel, Italy, Japan and Slovenia), it should be kept in mind that self-reporting might understate the influence of fiscal pressures[7]. In this same vein, most countries report extraordinary dividends as rare or non-existent, and most reported instances of extraordinary dividend pay-outs occurred in cases of excess capitalisation and strong financial performance of specific SOEs (in Canada, Estonia, Lithuania, the Netherlands, Poland and Switzerland). It bears mentioning that for fully incorporated SOEs subject to ordinary company law, in most countries shareholders are prohibited from proposing an increase in the normal dividend directly at the annual general meeting; any negotiations regarding dividend levels for such SOEs must therefore take place via prior consultations between the state and SOE boards.

Providing direct state support

Whereas excessive dividend pay-outs can threaten the commercial viability of SOEs, state subsidies (effectively an equivalent transaction in the opposite direction) act as a source of cheap capital, conferring a commercial advantage. Maintaining competitive neutrality between SOEs and private competitors does not mean that SOEs should not receive state support. Indeed, in addition to their purely commercial activities, SOEs are frequently faced with non-trivial public policy obligations. Adequately compensating SOEs for such obligations is important to ensure that they are not at a competitive disadvantage in the pursuit of their commercial aims. In order to ensure that state support does not constitute a departure from competitive neutrality, it should be calibrated to the additional cost that the public policy obligations impose on the SOE. Correctly attributing this cost can be facilitated by a clear structural separation between an SOE's commercial and non-commercial activities.

Beyond being relevant for countries committed to upholding competitive neutrality, state support is explicitly prohibited in European Union (and, by extension, the European Economic Area) member states. According to the Treaty on the Functioning of the European Union, member states are prohibited from providing "any aid [...] in any form whatsoever which distorts or threatens to distort competition by favouring certain undertakings or the production of certain goods [...]". However, state support in compensation for the discharge of public service obligations can be provided under certain conditions. The Altmark Criteria established by the EU Court of Justice detail the conditions under which state support may not be considered state aid, notably: if provided in return for public service obligations; if the procedures for calculating the compensation are established in advance; and if the compensation level does not exceed the amount necessary to cover the costs of the public service obligation and a reasonable profit. Additionally, the European Commission's Service of General Economic Interest (SGEI) package comprises a number of texts adopted by the Commission which further define the conditions under which state support can be considered compatible with EU rules[8].

The conditions surrounding state support in respondent countries can be broadly summarised as follows. In countries that do offer state support to SOEs, it can take several forms, including (i) direct capital injections in parallel with increases in equity; (ii) outright subsidies in compensation for the cost attributed to public service obligations, which are often governed by public service agreements; and, less frequently (iii) reductions in rate-of return requirements for SOEs engaged in both commercial and non-commercial activities. The latter form is notably the case in Lithuania (see details in Box 5). In principle, reductions in rate-of-return requirements can also take the form of lower dividend requirements, although this was not specifically reported in responses[9]. National practices regarding direct state support are also outlined in Table 4 and include:

1. *State support for public service obligations.* The vast majority of respondent countries report that state support for SOEs does occur. In these cases it is usually provided to a specific subset of companies (or a single company) primarily in compensation for the fulfilment of public service obligations (Australia, Canada, Chile, Estonia, Germany, Hungary, Ireland, Italy, Lithuania, the Netherlands, New Zealand, Norway, Poland, Sweden, Switzerland and the United Kingdom)[10]. Box 6 provides two examples from Canada on how specific SOEs are compensated for the fulfilment of public service obligations.

2. *State support not linked to public service obligations.* A few countries provide state support to SOEs but do not report that it is specifically for funding public service obligations (Israel, where support is reportedly rare; and Japan, where support is provided to state-owned airport companies). Where such support occurs it is sometimes justified by a need to overcome, or remedy, economic market failure.

3. *State support not provided.* In a minority of countries, state support is reportedly not provided to SOEs (Czech Republic, Finland and Slovenia). As mentioned above, EU member countries are subject to the EU state aid rules which prohibit any support that would distort competition or be against the general interest.

Box 5. **Financing SOEs' public service obligations in Lithuania**

SOEs in Lithuania receive state support primarily for the fulfilment of special (public service) obligations. Special obligations can be financed in a number of ways: (i) some SOEs are required to cover losses from special obligations from other activities (cross financing); (ii) some receive a cost refund from the public budget in compensation for the fulfilment of public service obligations; and (iii) some are entitled to cost plus moderate profit refund from public budget.

As SOEs perform special obligations which in most cases are loss making and do not receive full cost coverage, the required rate-of-return for these SOEs is set lower compared to rivals from the private sector. In 2013 it is expected that the government will pass a resolution requiring all SOEs to prepare and publish financial reports on ordinary commercial operations and special obligations separately. After measuring the significance of special obligations, the Governance Coordination Centre of the State Property Fund intends to propose to the government to set higher required rates of return on SOEs' commercial operations which would be comparable to the private sector.

Source: Submission by Lithuanian authorities in response to OECD questionnaire.

Box 6. **Conditions of direct state support for SOEs in Canada**

Every Canadian Crown corporation has been established for the purpose of pursuing a public policy objective. Canadian Crown corporations may be either self-sustaining, appropriations dependent, or both. Crown corporations may receive public funds in order to pursue their legislated mandate or priorities established by Cabinet or Parliament. Whether state support is provided on a one-time or on-going basis, it requires Parliamentary approval. This is required not only to seek the required funding but to establish the terms and conditions by which the corporation warrants government subvention. Through its responsible minister, the corporation must go through three major steps in order to access public funds: Cabinet approval, Treasury Board approval, and Parliamentary approval. Two examples of Crown corporations that receive State support in the form of direct parliamentary appropriations are elaborated below.

VIA Rail Canada: VIA receives parliamentary appropriations in order to fulfil its mandate "To manage and provide a safe and efficient passenger rail service." While VIA collects revenue from its operations, the parliamentary appropriations offset the difference between its revenue and the cost of providing its service in pursuit of its mandate. Parliamentary appropriations have also been used to help VIA realise its mandate through the purchase of rolling stock, etc. See VIA's annual report (http://www.viarail.ca/en/about-via-rail/our-company/annual-reports/annual-report-2012) for more information.

Canada Post: Canada Post receives parliamentary appropriations to cover the costs of providing services which would not otherwise be self-supporting, namely, mailing privileges for the Governor General, members of Parliament and other offices of Parliament, mail for the blind, and the library book rate.

Source: Submission by Canadian authorities in response to OECD questionnaire.

Table 4. **National practices regarding state support for SOEs**

State support for public service obligations	**Australia:** SOEs may receive grants to fund the delivery of public service obligations ("Community Service Obligations" in the national nomenclature). They can also receive compensation for price obligations imposed on SOEs that supply public goods and services in a monopolistic market. **Canada:** There is no overall principle setting out the conditions for according state support to SOEs. All SOEs in Canada are established to fulfil some form of public policy objective, and are either financially self-sustaining, dependent on government appropriations or a mixture of both. Some examples of state support accorded to SOEs occur in the cases of the railway company VIA Rail Canada and the postal company Canada Post, which both regularly receive parliamentary appropriations to fund activities that are not financially self-sustaining (e.g. Canada Post offers the mailing of letters free of charge between citizens and certain governmental bodies). In addition to capital appropriations, capital injections in exchange for equity shares are also possible. Whether state support to SOEs is time-bound or on-going, it requires approval from the government Cabinet, the Treasury Board and the Parliament. **Chile:** There is no general mechanism shaping the conditions for state support. Support can take the form of capital injections or ordinary transfers, which are usually administered via the passing of dedicated laws. There are examples of direct transfers provided to transport companies in exchange for the delivery of public service obligations. There is currently a draft law in congress which would fix a dedicated annual state transfer to the State Trains Company (EFE) in compensation for ensuring the delivery of public transportation services. **Estonia:** Direct state support is primarily offered to SOEs responsible for fulfilling public service obligations. The two examples provided involve an SOE primarily engaged in the dismantling of nuclear sites (AS A.L.A.R.A) and a transport SOE (AS Elektriraudtee). The latter company has a monopoly on passenger rail operations in Estonia. State support for Elektriraudtee takes the form of a capital transfer equal to the part of the company's operating costs not covered by ticket revenue. Generally, direct state support takes the form of capital transfers which appear in the companies' income statements as single-purpose revenue for a specific activity. The authorities do not consider capital injections in return for increased equity to be a form of state support. **Germany:** Most SOEs owned by the federal level of government do not receive state support. The only current exception involves support for the construction and maintenance of the country railway network, for which the federal government is legally responsible. This support takes the form of direct capital transfers or interest-free loans. **Hungary:** SOEs may receive direct state support to fund public service obligations, in accordance with the EU regulations governing state aid. In some cases, the conditions for state support are defined by dedicated public service agreements signed between the SOE and the relevant ministry(ies). **Ireland:** The state-owned transport company CIE receives exchequer grants to fund public service obligations, paid under a contract with an independent regulator who monitors their delivery. The grants are paid in accordance with the relevant EU regulations governing state aid.

	Italy: Direct state support for SOEs does occur. Support takes the form of capital injections to finance investments and maintenance in rail and road, or direct transfers to compensate for public service obligations. In the latter case, public service agreements between SOEs and the relevant ministry(ies) are used. **Korea:** State support is provided to SOEs primarily in compensation for public service delivery, including the interest costs associated with financing projects commissioned by the government. State support can take several forms, including: (i) equity investments; (ii) direct capital transfers; and (iii) provision of loans. For large-scale or long-term projects, equity investments and debt financing are the main forms of state support used. **Lithuania:** State support is provided to SOEs to finance public service obligations, including through: (i) cross-financing by SOEs from commercial activities to non-commercial activities; (ii) direct compensation for the provision of public service obligations; and (iii) direct compensation for the provision of public service obligations, based on cost plus moderate profit. SOEs do not report separately on commercial and non-commercial activities in Lithuania, which complicates the dedicated financing of their public service obligations. It is estimated that these compensation mechanisms do not fully offset the cost of SOEs' public service obligations, and as a result the government requires that SOEs achieve an overall rate-of-return that is lower than their private sector competitors. **Netherlands:** Direct state support for SOEs is rare. If the authorities do grant state support, it is subject to the "private investor principle", meaning that the state requires a compensation for guarantees, loans and equity that is consistent with the requirements of private investors. Additionally, the Ministry of Finance is consulted if support represents the potential risk of being considered state aid. In 2011 and 2012, the government provided a cash transfer to the electricity provider Tennet to fulfil investments in infrastructure required by the Electricity Act. **New Zealand:** State support for SOEs is rare, although a provision in the SOE Act allows for the government to request non-commercial services from SOEs. New Zealand Railways Corporation (KiwiRail) recently received an exceptional capital injection (via an equity increase) to fund the rebuilding of essential infrastructure. There is no immediate expected return on this investment, but the ten-year plan on which the investment was made forecasts that the company will ultimately generate self-sustaining profits. **Norway:** The majority of SOEs under the purview of the ownership Ministry are commercial companies which are not liable to receive direct state support. However, some SOEs with sectoral policy objectives, such as hospitals and certain airports, do receive state support, most commonly in the form of yearly capital grants from the central government. The direct support complies with the requirements outlined in the Agreement on the European Economic Area (EEA Agreement). **Poland:** SOEs that are wholly-owned by the treasury and that fulfil public service obligations can receive direct state support other than public aid. Examples of this include: the Polish Press Agency, which receives an annual state subsidy; two salt mines that receive state subsidies to close certain mining facilities and preserve their historical sections; and Spa Company, which received a capital injection from the state in return for new equity issues.

	Sweden: State support for SOEs is rare, and would be subject to EU regulations governing state aid. When state support is provided, it is for the purpose of funding special tasks and public service obligations, and generally takes the form of capital appropriations. **Switzerland:** SOEs do not generally receive direct state support, even when they are delivering public service obligations. The only case of instance of direct state support occurs in the case of SBB (Federal Railways), which receives subsidies for investment in railway infrastructure. In case state support was requested by an SOE, the parliament would have the responsibility of making the decision to accord the support. **United Kingdom:** Most SOEs operating commercially do not receive direct funding from the state. One exception is the Green Investment Bank, which was established in 2012 to provide funding to sustainable energy infrastructure projects. Green Investment Bank currently receives direct cash injections from the government to finance its activities. It is expected that government funding will gradually be replaced with funding from other sources.
State support not linked to public service obligations	**Israel:** SOEs generally do not benefit from direct state support and they are required to operate on a commercial basis, under the same business considerations as privately-owned companies. Additionally, any SOE transactions which would restrict the government in exercising its functions require prior government approval, for which the process is outlined in the Government Companies Law (see Box 1). In a limited number of cases and under exceptional circumstances, SOEs have received state support in the following forms: loan guarantees; direct state loans and loan concessions; and the postponement of loan payments in return for additional shares. **Japan:** Direct state support is provided to state-owned airport companies in the form of subsidies (direct capital transfers). The process is as follows: airport companies submit a subsidy request to the Minister of Land, Infrastructure, Transport and Tourism, who examines the request. The decision to provide support to airport companies is based on forecasts regarding the SOE's future financial performance. (Direct support for state-owned expressway companies has not been considered.)
State support not provided	In **Czech Republic**, state support to SOEs is prohibited by law, in accordance with EU regulations governing state aid. In **Finland**, SOEs operating commercially do not benefit from state support. In cases where direct state support would be considered, it would be subject to EU regulations governing state aid. In **Slovenia**, SOEs do not benefit from direct state support.

Source: Submissions by national authorities in response to OECD questionnaire.

Conclusion: National models for SOE financing

As shown in the precedent sections, there are large differences across respondent countries in the level of policy development regarding SOE financing as well as the respective roles of the state and SOE boards in making financing decisions. Based on the national practices reported so far, three SOE financing "models" suggest themselves (summarised in Table 5).

Table 5. **Overview of national models relating to SOE capital structure decisions**

	Country	Explicit capital structure guidelines	Rate-of-return targets	Guiding principles or targets for dividend levels	Direct state support to SOEs possible
Well-defined capital structure guidelines inform subsequent financing decisions	**Australia**	Yes	Yes	Yes – general guidelines	Yes
	Estonia	Yes	Yes	No	Yes
	Ireland	Yes, for large SOEs	No	Yes – explicit targets	Yes
	Netherlands	Yes	Yes	Yes – general guidelines and explicit minimum targets	Yes
	New Zealand	Yes	Yes	Yes – general guidelines	Yes
	Norway	Yes, general guidelines	Yes	Yes – explicit targets	Yes
	Sweden	Yes	Yes	Yes	Yes
	Switzerland	Yes	Yes	Yes – explicit targets	Yes
	United Kingdom	Yes, although not uniform across entire SOE sector	Yes	Yes – general guidelines and explicit targets, varies by SOE	Yes – reportedly rare for commercial SOEs
Financial targets established in some cases	**Canada**	Yes, indirectly through financial risk management guidelines	Yes	No	Yes
	Chile	No	Yes	No	Yes
	Hungary	No	Yes	No	Yes
	Lithuania	No	Yes	Yes – explicit targets	Yes
	Poland	No	No	Yes – general guidelines	Yes
	Slovenia	No	No	Yes – explicit targets	No
Financial decisions made on a case-by-case basis	**Czech Republic**	No	No	No	No
	Finland	No	No	No	No
	Germany	No	No	No	Yes
	Israel	No	No	Yes – general guidelines	Yes – in exceptional cases
	Italy	No	No	No	Yes
	Japan	No	No	No	Yes

Source: Submissions by national authorities in response to OECD questionnaire.

3. Sources and conditions of SOE financing

Recapitalising SOEs

Recapitalisation – significant changes in a company's capital structure – can take a number of forms, including (i) the issuance and purchase of new equity shares (capital injections); (ii) the provision of capital without a corresponding increase in equity shares (capital transfers) or (iii) a significant change in the relative balance of debt and equity (e.g. leveraged recapitalisations). For SOEs in particular, the possible motivations behind recapitalisations vary and include: capital injections or transfers to finance time-bound investment projects (e.g. construction of new railway infrastructure) or to shore up failing companies[11]; recurrent capital transfers in compensation for the fulfilment of public service obligations; and changes to the capital structure balance to prepare the SOE for privatisation (e.g. reducing the debt/equity ratio in the case of highly leveraged SOEs) or to prevent a hostile takeover (e.g. increasing the debt/equity ratio to make the firm less attractive to the interested investor)[12].

To maintain a level playing field with private competitors, the conditions of SOE recapitalisations should be consistent with private sector practices. This is notably important regarding the cost of capital attributed to SOE recapitalisations. When SOE recapitalisations occur without corresponding increases in equity (i.e. in the form of subsidies), or in the absence of minimum forecasted commercial returns on the investment, then SOEs are effectively receiving equity financing at lower than market rates. To ensure market consistent equity costs, the authorities can require that recapitalisations from the public budget can only occur following the demonstration of a minimum forecasted return on equity, in line with private sector standards (this would apply specifically to the commercial activities of the concerned SOE).

Regarding the process and conditions for SOE recapitalisations, country practices can be summarised as follows (see also section on "Establishing rate-of-return requirements", which notably provides information on return-on-equity requirements that would presumably apply to cases of SOE recapitalisation). Further details are provided in Table 6.

1. *Recent SOE recapitalisations.* Regarding recent SOE recapitalisations, there are two groups of respondents:

   – In the majority of respondent countries, SOE recapitalisations from the public budget can and do occur. Common stock is the predominant form of equity instrument used. In some cases, subordinated debt or convertible bonds are also used to recapitalise (Finland and Slovenia, respectively). In one country, the contribution of shares from one SOE to another was cited as one means of recapitalisation (Poland).

   – In a small group of countries, questionnaire responses report either that there are no recent examples of SOE recapitalisation (Czech Republic, Germany, Japan and Switzerland) or that they are rare (Finland, New Zealand, Sweden and the United Kingdom)[13]. In two countries (Ireland and Italy), SOE recapitalisations from the public budget reportedly do not occur.

2. *Involving minority shareholders.* Among the countries that provided information on the involvement of minority shareholders in the recapitalisation decision and process, most reported that minority shareholders are invited to participate in new share issues in proportion to their original ownership share. One country (Poland) reports that subscription rights on new capital issues can be denied to existing shareholders if deemed in the ultimate interest of the company. In another country (Korea), minority shareholders are generally not involved in the recapitalisation decision and process.

3. *Ensuring market consistent equity costs.* The large majority of respondent countries report that when recapitalising wholly-owned, unlisted SOEs, there are no mechanisms in place to ensure that the cost of capital is market consistent[14]. However, five countries report an interesting practice, whereby recapitalisations from the public budget can only be accorded via capital injection to projects that demonstrate a minimum expected rate-of-return (Australia, Estonia, Hungary, New Zealand and Sweden). In these cases, methodologies for demonstrating the expected return vary. With the exception of Estonia and Hungary, these minimum return requirements are communicated to SOEs through the authorities' ownership guidelines[15]. In Norway, a similar practice occurs whereby the terms of new equity issues are subject to a review by independent financial advisors.

Table 6. **Conditions and process for SOE recapitalisations**

Recapitalisations from the public budget subject to minimum expected rate-of-return	**Australia:** Two start-up companies are currently being recapitalised from the public budget: NBN Co. and the Moorebank Intermodal Company. Equity is being issued in the form of ordinary shares. Regarding the involvement of minority shareholders in recapitalisations, Snowy Hydro is referenced as an SOE that is not wholly-owned by the central government (it is also owned by the New South Wales and Victorian State Governments). The company's constitution establishes that any decisions related to the increase or decrease in share capital must be approved by unanimous resolution of its members. In cases of equity issuance for wholly-owned unlisted SOEs, ensuring market consistency of the cost of capital is enshrined in the Government Business Enterprise Guidelines, which stipulate that SOEs should earn a commercial rate-of-return and recover the cost of all resources employed, including the cost of capital. In the case of the recapitalisation of NBN Co., the company has developed a comprehensive business case in support of its recapitalisation and has demonstrated a forecasted internal rate-of-return of 7.1%. **Estonia:** SOE recapitalisations from the public budget do occur. When they take the form of increases in share capital, ordinary shares are usually used. (In the case of one real estate SOE, AS Riigi Kinnisvara, state recapitalisations take the form of annual increases in share capital in exchange for transfers of state property to the company). In recapitalisation cases where the state is not the sole owner of an SOE, all shareholders may participate in new capital issues in proportion to their ownership share. In cases of equity issuance for wholly-owned unlisted SOEs, the state will only provide a capital injection upon demonstration of projected improvements in financial performance, and under the expectation that profitability will be comparable to private competitors. (See Box 2 for details on how return on equity is calculated in Estonia.) **Hungary:** For SOE recapitalisations where the state is not the sole owner, Hungarian law requires majority shareholders to invite minority shareholders to participate in new capital issues. Most recapitalisations take the form of common stock. When issuing equity for wholly-owned unlisted SOEs, the cost of capital is subject to a review by the TV1 (State Aid Monitoring Office) in accordance with EU rules. Under these rules, capital increases must respect market standards. **New Zealand:** SOE recapitalisations are rare in practice, but according to New Zealand's ownership expectations manual, they are possible in cases of severe underperformance. To date, there have been no recapitalisation cases involving minority shareholders. In cases of equity issuance for wholly-owned unlisted SOEs, there is a stringent requirement that projected returns exceed the cost of capital. An exceptional recapitalisation case involved New Zealand Railways Corporation (KiwiRail), where the government injected capital for infrastructure rebuilding. There is no immediate expected return on this investment, but self-sustaining profits are forecasted in the ten-year plan. **Norway:** SOE recapitalisations from the public budget do occur, generally taking the form of common stock. In cases of equity issuance for wholly-owned unlisted SOEs, the ownership Ministry seeks an

	independent opinion from professional financial advisors on the terms of the equity issue and its strategic and financial motivations. According to the state support policy, the state can only participate in a rights issue if grounded in a commercial rationale. **Sweden:** SOE recapitalisations from the public budget are rare, and when they do occur they generally take the form of common stock. A few recent instances have involved rights issues rather than equity issues, and minority shareholders enjoyed equal rights to participate. When issuing equity for wholly-owned unlisted SOEs, a calculation of its cost of capital is made based on estimated risk of the investment. The equity is issued if the SOE can add economic value (if the estimated return on investment is positive).
No mechanisms in place to ensure market consistent cost of equity financing	**Chile:** Recapitalisations from the public budget can only occur following approval by Congress, either through dedicated legislation or inclusion in the annual Budget Law. Two companies, Metro S.A. and SAISPA SpA., are recapitalised on a regular basis through the budget law. Extraordinary recapitalisations in the form of direct capital transfers have occurred in CODELCO (2009), ENAP (2008) and BECH (2009), all authorised by case-specific laws. There have been no cases of recapitalisations involving minority shareholders in unlisted companies; for listed companies with minority shareholders, recapitalisation decisions are made in shareholders meetings. In cases of equity issuance for wholly-owned unlisted SOEs, no mechanisms are in place to ensure that the cost of capital is market consistent. **Finland:** SOE recapitalisations from the public budget have occurred in the past but are very infrequent. When they do occur, recapitalisations normally take the form of common stock or subordinated debt. Since the creation of the country's dedicated ownership function within the Prime Minister's Office (the Ownership Steering Department), only two SOE recapitalisations from the public budget have occurred. In both instances, the concerned SOEs had been recently established from existing in-house activities of ministries. The recapitalisations occurred shortly after SOE establishment when it was determined that the companies were undercapitalised. There have been no examples of recapitalisations involving minority shareholders, but if such a case were to occur, minority shareholders would be consulted in advance of the annual shareholders' meeting and be invited, as all shareholders, to participate in new capital issues in proportion to their ownership share. In cases of equity issuance for wholly-owned unlisted SOEs, no mechanisms are in place to ensure that the cost of capital is market consistent. **Israel:** There have been recent cases of SOE recapitalisations, generally involving allocation of regular shares. In instances of recapitalisation for SOEs that are not wholly-owned by the government, other shareholders are consulted in advance in order to achieve shareholder agreement regarding changes in share capital. In cases of equity issuance for wholly-owned unlisted SOEs, no mechanisms are in place to ensure that the cost of capital is market consistent; equity is issued according to acceptable business standards. **Korea:** During the past five years, SOE recapitalisations from the public budget have occurred in a few wholly state-owned unlisted companies,

	notably Korea Land and Housing Corporation and Korea National Oil Corporation, both in support of public policy objectives. Government recapitalisations generally take the form of common stock issuance. Minority shareholders are generally not involved in the SOE recapitalisation decision and process. When recapitalising wholly-owned unlisted SOEs, there is no specific mechanism to ensure market-consistent equity costs. However, capital issuance for SOE establishment is subject to a feasibility study, followed by annual reviews of financial performance and impact on the public budget during five years. **Lithuania:** In cases of SOE recapitalisations from the public budget, the main form of equity used is common shares. The government as a shareholder does not generally consult with minority owners in advance of recapitalisation decisions, but they are invited to participate in new equity issues on a pro rata basis. In cases of equity issuance for wholly-owned unlisted SOEs, no mechanisms are in place to ensure that the cost of capital is market consistent. New projects that are candidates for recapitalisation undergo a financial sustainability analysis on a case by case basis. When estimating expected returns over cost of capital, the government takes into account both the expected financial return and public interest considerations. **Netherlands:** The only reported recent example of recapitalisation of a non-financial SOE involved a capital injection of €600 million to the electricity network operator Tennet in 2012. Common equity was used. The cost of capital was assessed by an independent regulator because Tennet is a regulated entity. Generally, in cases of equity issuance for wholly-owned unlisted SOEs, no mechanisms are currently in place to ensure that the cost of capital is market consistent. However, the authorities are in the process of developing a policy to establish market consistent benchmark returns for individual SOEs. **Poland:** Recapitalisations from the public budget primarily take the form of (i) a contribution of shares from one company to another or (ii) acquisition of newly issued shares by the state, in accordance with EU regulations. Decisions to recapitalise are made at the annual general meeting. Existing shareholders generally have the right to participate in new capital subscriptions in proportion to their original ownership share. However, a decision can be made at the general meeting to deny all or part of shareholders' subscription rights if in the company's interest. This can take place upon proposal by the management board, accompanied with a written opinion justifying the proposal and suggesting a new share issue price, or its method of calculation. In cases of equity issuance for wholly-owned unlisted SOEs, no mechanisms are in place to ensure that the cost of capital is market consistent. The issue price of new shares is determined at the general meeting. According to questionnaire responses, the issue price is determined on market terms. **Slovenia:** The only reported recent recapitalisations have involved state-owned banks. Common stock is generally the predominant equity instrument used, but in the recent cases convertible bonds were issued and later converted into stocks. Generally, the decision to recapitalise must be approved by company members, and minority shareholders are usually invited to participate in the process. In cases of equity issuance for wholly-owned unlisted SOEs, mechanisms are in place to ensure that

	the cost of capital is market consistent; equity issuance is only done for reasons of public or state interest. **United Kingdom:** For the vast majority of SOEs, recapitalisations from the public budget do not occur. The Green Investment Bank is one exception. It receives direct capital injections to finance its activities. As it expands its portfolio of investments, new capital will continue to be provided by the state, although it is not expected that this funding model be pursued indefinitely.
SOE recapitalisations from the public budget do not occur	**Ireland; Italy; Japan; Germany** (no recent examples of recapitalisations of non-financial SOEs via new equity issues); **Czech Republic** (no cases of SOE recapitalisations from the public budget in recent years); **Switzerland** (there have not been any recapitalisations since the SOEs were externalised from the federal administration 15 years ago).

Source: Submissions by national authorities in response to OECD questionnaire.

Financing through debt

Where SOEs operate commercially and with limited government involvement in operational and managerial decisions, the authorities do not always have detailed knowledge of SOE practices regarding debt financing. However, most respondent countries have been able to provide some general information on the extent to which SOEs access debt financing from the commercial marketplace and/or from government institutions, as well as the main forms of debt financing used in the most commonly occurring cases. According to questionnaire responses, the main sources and forms of debt financing for SOEs can be summarised as follows:

1. *Commercial debt financing*. SOEs in the majority of respondent countries access debt financing uniquely in the commercial marketplace. In a handful of countries, this practice is enshrined in legal provisions prohibiting SOEs from accessing debt financing from government agencies (Chile and Sweden). The main reported debt instruments used are as follows:

   – *Commercial loans*. In all countries where information was available, the primary form of debt financing used by SOEs is commercial loans.

   – *Tradable bonds*. Several countries report that some large SOEs also use tradable bonds, notably when financing is needed for large scale and/or long-term investment projects (Chile, Ireland, Israel, Japan, the Netherlands, Sweden and Switzerland). This is to be expected, as large companies with perceived growth opportunities are obviously more attractive for potential investors.

- *Private placements*. One country reports that private placements are a frequent form of debt financing used by some larger SOEs (Ireland).

2. *Government debt financing*. In a smaller group of countries, some specific SOEs (or groups of SOEs) are able to borrow directly from government institutions, either via treasury loans or from state-owned financial institutions.

   - *Treasury loans*. In a small group of countries, it is possible for some specific SOEs to access debt financing directly from government agencies (this is the case for specific SOEs in Australia, Canada, Estonia, Germany, Japan, the Netherlands, Switzerland and the United Kingdom). In two countries, debt financing from government agencies is available to a broader group of SOEs under certain conditions (Hungary and Poland). In the United Kingdom, all SOEs are required to obtain debt financing uniquely from government sources.

   - *Loans from state-owned financial institutions*. One country (Germany) reports that while SOEs cannot borrow from the state treasury, they can borrow from state-owned financial institutions. However, most countries did not provide specific reporting on the provision of loans by state-owned banks. This is mostly a consequence of the fact that state-owned financial institutions (except for niche operators such as export-import banks) are increasingly rare. Moreover, such state-owned banks as do still operate in the marketplace are increasingly considered as standard commercial lenders. Collection of targeted information on the conditions of loans offered by state-owned banks to SOEs would be necessary to assess the impact of state ownership on lending practices.

Table 7 provides an overview of questionnaire responses concerning the main sources and forms of debt financing, as well as information on the terms and conditions of such debt, where such information was provided. The section that follows describes in greater detail the terms and conditions associated with SOE debt financing in respondent countries, including the conditions surrounding state guarantees and government debt financing, as well as a discussion of mechanisms to neutralise preferential financing terms for SOEs.

Table 7. Overview of main sources and forms of debt financing for SOEs

Country	Source(s) of SOE debt financing	Main debt instruments	Conditions for state guarantees on debt	Preferential terms for commercial loans?	Debt neutrality mechanisms	Off-market funding mechanisms from other SOEs?
Australia	Marketplace. Exception for Defence Housing Australia, which borrows solely from the government.	Commercial loans. Bond issuance is avoided, to avoid the conflicting information provision requirements between the Government Business Enterprise Guidelines and the Corporations Act[16].	No guarantees as a general rule.	No	Yes. For SOEs borrowing from the government, debt neutrality adjustments are incorporated in the cost of debt. For SOEs borrowing from the marketplace, state ownership guidelines stipulate that they are to put in place a capital structure with a view to achieving an investment grade credit rating (not the credit rating of the government). The current target is BBB.	No

Country	Source(s) of SOE debt financing	Main debt instruments	Conditions for state guarantees on debt	Preferential terms for commercial loans?	Debt neutrality mechanisms	Off-market funding mechanisms from other SOEs?
Canada	Marketplace. Exception for four SOEs, which can also receive loans from the state treasury.	Commercial loans. Larger SOEs may also issue bonds, while smaller SOEs rely primarily on commercial loans.	Explicit guarantees effectively (although not explicitly) accorded to SOEs considered "agents of the Crown". Other SOEs reportedly may benefit from an implicit state guarantee.	Yes, it is considered possible that commercial lenders offer credit on favourable terms owing to a perceived, or implicit, state guarantee.	No	Yes, off-market funding mechanisms are permitted by the Crown Corporation General Regulations. Their use requires prior approval from the Minister of Finance, including approval of timing, terms and conditions. The use of such mechanisms is infrequent.
Chile	Marketplace. SOEs prohibited by law from accessing loans from government agencies and other SOEs.	Primarily commercial loans. Larger SOEs also issue bonds in international and domestic markets.	Guarantees can be provided to specific SOEs upon request to the Ministry of Finance.	Yes, it is considered likely that commercial lenders perceive that state ownership reduces the credit risk of SOEs.	No	No, supplier and trade credits between SOEs are prohibited by the Chilean constitution.
Czech Republic	Marketplace		No state guarantees	No	No	

Country	Source(s) of SOE debt financing	Main debt instruments	Conditions for state guarantees on debt	Preferential terms for commercial loans?	Debt neutrality mechanisms	Off-market funding mechanisms from other SOEs?
Estonia	Marketplace. Exceptions in the past for Estonian Air and Port of Tallinn, which have received loans from the state treasury.	Primarily bonds (69% of all debt financing to SOEs), followed by commercial loans.	No state guarantees	Yes, change-of-control clauses reportedly included in the loan covenants of some large SOEs. In some cases, such clauses stipulate a cancellation of the loan contract in case of change in control. However, no analysis has been done on the extent to which preferential terms (e.g. lower interest rate due to strong credit rating) are due to ownership or company characteristics such as size, client base, etc.	No. For loans offered to specific SOEs by the state treasury, mechanism in place to ensure market consistent interest rate.	No, commercial and supplier credits between SOEs are prohibited by the Chilean Constitution.
Finland	Marketplace		No state guarantees	No. Change-of-control clauses are reportedly typical, but no information is available on how state ownership influences commercial banks' practices with regards to change-of-control clauses.	No	Same practices as private competitors.

Country	Source(s) of SOE debt financing	Main debt instruments	Conditions for state guarantees on debt	Preferential terms for commercial loans?	Debt neutrality mechanisms	Off-market funding mechanisms from other SOEs?
Germany	Marketplace, including state-owned financial institutions active on the marketplace[17]. Exception for Deutsche Bahn AG, which has received interest-free loans from the government.		Guarantees possible for state-owned and private banks, and SOEs with sectoral policy objectives.	No	No	
Hungary	Primarily marketplace, but debt financing from government institutions and other SOEs also possible.	Primarily commercial loans. Tradable bonds not commonly used.	No state guarantees for SOEs under the portfolio of Hungarian National Assets Management		Government and SOE loans are reviewed for market consistency by the State Aid Monitoring Office in accordance with EU regulations on state aid.	Same practices as private competitors.
Ireland	Marketplace.	Primarily commercial loans. Larger SOEs also use tradable bonds. Some SOEs also use private placements, particularly in the U.S. market.	No state guarantees	No (except that commercial banks might perceive that SOEs have a lower risk of default owing to their government ownership)	No (not aware of any mechanisms)	Same practices as private competitors.

Country	Source(s) of SOE debt financing	Main debt instruments	Conditions for state guarantees on debt	Preferential terms for commercial loans?	Debt neutrality mechanisms	Off-market funding mechanisms from other SOEs?
Israel	Marketplace. In exceptional cases, direct loans from state treasury are possible. The state can also in exceptional cases postpone the payment of existing loans in exchange for additional shares, or offer concession of loans.	Primarily commercial loans and traded bonds. Traded bonds encouraged by government to foster transparency and accountability of SOEs.	No guarantees as a general rule, but exceptional cases have occurred.	No (except that SOEs might receive higher credit ratings than private firms, according to generally accepted norms of rating agencies)	No	Information not available. Practices considered likely to be similar to private sector.
Japan	Marketplace and government institutions for some state-owned airport companies. Marketplace for state-owned expressway companies.	Commercial loans for short-term financing needs; bonds for long-term. For airport companies that borrow from marketplace and government, government loans used for large investments in plant and machinery.	Guarantees possible for state-owned airport companies.		No. Government loans for state-owned airport companies are subject to an interest rate equal to the rate on government bonds plus a margin.	No for state-owned airport companies. Information not available for state-owned expressway companies.

Country	Source(s) of SOE debt financing	Main debt instruments	Conditions for state guarantees on debt	Preferential terms for commercial loans?	Debt neutrality mechanisms	Off-market funding mechanisms from other SOEs?
Korea	Marketplace	Primarily commercial loans. Corporate bonds for projects that require large-scale investments, such as national property development.				SOEs access trade credits from banks following similar practices as private competitors. Information not provided on the use of supplier and trade credits between SOEs.
Lithuania	Marketplace	Primarily commercial loans; no recent cases of bond issuance.	No state guarantees		No	Information not available. Practices considered likely to be similar to private sector.
Netherlands	Marketplace and (partially) state-owned banks, on commercial terms.	Primarily commercial loans. Large SOEs also issue tradable bonds for large investments.	State guarantees possible only for financial institutions and for Dutch Railways when accessing loans from Eurofima, subject to a commercial fee.	Yes. Information not available on private loan conditions for SOEs, but considered likely to be preferential. Rating agencies apply higher credit ratings to SOEs.	No	Information not available (no policy on the use of off-market financing mechanisms).

Country	Source(s) of SOE debt financing	Main debt instruments	Conditions for state guarantees on debt	Preferential terms for commercial loans?	Debt neutrality mechanisms	Off-market funding mechanisms from other SOEs?
New Zealand	Marketplace. Exception for New Zealand Railways Corporation (KiwiRail) has historically been able to access debt financing from the treasury, benefitting from a state guarantee.	Primarily commercial loans. Tradable bonds have been used in a few recent cases. Detailed information on their relative importance not available.	No state guarantees. Exception for NZ Railways Corporation (KiwiRail) whose establishment legislation provided for state guarantees on commercial debt. Such guarantees no longer possible, but still apply to previously-contracted debt.	No	No	Information not available. Practices considered likely to be similar to private sector.
Norway	Marketplace.	Primarily commercial loans. Some larger SOES use tradable debt instruments.	No state guarantees, as stipulated by law and in accordance with the EEA (European Economic Area) Agreement	Information not available on the terms of private loans to SOEs, but reported evidence that rating agencies apply higher credit ratings to SOEs.		No (according to information available to the reporting entity)

Country	Source(s) of SOE debt financing	Main debt instruments	Conditions for state guarantees on debt	Preferential terms for commercial loans?	Debt neutrality mechanisms	Off-market funding mechanisms from other SOEs?
Poland	Marketplace and government institutions.	Practices similar to private sector.	Yes, guarantees can be provided to SOEs, but are also available for private companies. Reporting entity did not have access to information on the application procedures or conditions for state guarantees.	No		
Slovenia	Marketplace	Primarily commercial loans. In some cases, loans granted by International Financial Institutions.	State guarantees possible when deemed to be in the public interest, via dedicated legislation.	No	No	

Country	Source(s) of SOE debt financing	Main debt instruments	Conditions for state guarantees on debt	Preferential terms for commercial loans?	Debt neutrality mechanisms	Off-market funding mechanisms from other SOEs?
Sweden	Marketplace. SOEs prohibited from borrowing from government institutions.	Primarily commercial loans. Larger and some medium-sized SOEs also issue bonds.	No state guarantees	Yes. Banks loans have been offered on preferential terms. Recent cases of bond issuance by SOEs have been subject to preferential interest rates (50-75 basis points lower than private competitors.	No	No
Switzerland	Marketplace. Exception for Federal Railways SBB, which can receive loans from the treasury within certain limitations.	Both commercial loans and tradable bonds, depending on cost and financial need.	No state guarantees. Exceptions for sub national railway companies, which receive state guarantees to allow them to access financing at the same rates as Federal Railways SBB (which receives government loans).	No	No. Exception for government loans to Federal Railways SBB subject to an interest rate equal to the cost of debt for the government plus a commercial fee, to approximate market standards.	Information not available. Practices considered likely to be similar to private sector. Preferential debt conditions between SOEs would not be in line with the Federal Council's company-specific Strategic Objectives communicated every four years to SOEs.

Country	Source(s) of SOE debt financing	Main debt instruments	Conditions for state guarantees on debt	Preferential terms for commercial loans?	Debt neutrality mechanisms	Off-market funding mechanisms from other SOEs?
United Kingdom	Exclusively government debt financing for most SOEs, either via National Loans Fund or relevant shareholding department where loan terms are agreed with the treasury. Some reported exceptions include Green Investment Bank (could in principle access commercial debt financing); Urenco (minority-owned); and a few other SOEs for which the terms of commercial loans are established in advance via a Trading Fund Order.	Not applicable in most cases. However, minority-owned Urenco has a variety of forms of debt financing, including tradable bonds.	Not applicable	Not applicable	Government loans require presentation of a compelling business plan. When loans are provided to finance commercial activities, there is an expectation that they will be granted on commercial terms.	Not applicable

Source: Submissions by national authorities in response to OECD questionnaire.

Identifying the cost of debt financing

Whether SOE financing is obtained in the commercial marketplace and/or from government institutions, a departure from competitive neutrality can occur if the lender(s) offer financing at preferential terms as compared to private competitors. In the case of commercial lenders, they may perceive lower risk associated with SOE debt owing to implicit or explicit state guarantees, and price their loans accordingly. In the case of government lenders, they may offer loans at concessionary rates in order to support national champions, protect weak enterprises or encourage selected economic activities.

A number of possible mechanisms to neutralise such inadvertent cost advantages do exist, but few countries have put them in place. While the scope for government influence on the terms of commercial lending is arguably limited, the authorities can, for example, require SOEs to explicitly stipulate in commercial loan covenants that their debt does not carry a governmental guarantee (this is notably the case in New Zealand). Where SOEs can, or must, access financing from government sources, the authorities likely have greater ability to maintain costs at market consistent rates, for example by charging an interest rate that approximates the level of risk associated with the commercial activities of the SOE. Such arrangements can also strengthen transparency, both among competing enterprises and the broader public, regarding the financing costs faced by SOEs.

According to questionnaire responses, the conditions surrounding SOE debt financing in respondent countries can be summarised as follows:

1. *Government guarantees on loans*. In the majority of respondent countries, SOEs generally do not benefit from standing government guarantees on commercial debt. However, in almost half of respondent countries, explicit guarantees can be provided to specific SOEs or categories of SOEs (Canada, Chile, Germany, Israel, Japan, Netherlands, New Zealand, Poland, Slovenia and Switzerland). Box 7 provides an example from Israel on the provision on exceptional guarantees to SOEs. In countries where explicit government guarantees are possible, the conditions surrounding them are described in Table 8.
2. *Other preferential financing conditions*. Almost all countries report that there is no evidence that SOEs benefit from advantageous financing conditions on the commercial market. The exceptions are Canada, Chile, Estonia, Italy, Netherlands, Norway and Sweden, where questionnaire responses report that there is indeed evidence of preferential financing terms accorded to SOEs. While most respondent countries did not have information on the terms of SOEs' commercial debt, some reported that

credit rating agencies accord a higher rating to SOE debt owing to their state ownership. With the exception of Australia, no countries have put in place mechanisms to compensate for any potentially advantageous financing terms attached to commercial loans.

3. *Debt neutrality mechanisms.* The specific instances for which debt neutrality mechanisms have been established by the authorities are as follows:
   - *Commercial debt financing.* Australia is the only country where the authorities have put in place an explicit mechanism to ensure that all SOEs benefitting from concessionary financing on the commercial marketplace must pay a debt neutrality charge[18].
   - *Government debt financing.* The only other reported cases where mechanisms are in place to ensure market consistent loan terms occur for specific SOEs that access debt financing directly from government institutions. This applies to: SOEs borrowing from government institutions in Australia (in the form of a margin above the 10-year treasury rate); two SOEs in Estonia (in the form of an interest rate based on the state's cost of capital plus a risk premium); one SOE in Switzerland (in the form of an interest rate equal to the interest cost for the government, plus a commercial fee); and the majority SOEs in the United Kingdom. In countries where specific SOEs can access debt financing from government agencies, the terms of such financing are described in Table 9.

Box 7. **Exceptional state guarantees for SOEs in Israel**

As a rule, the State of Israel does not provide direct support, such as guarantees to SOEs. SOEs are required to operate in accordance with the same business considerations employed by non-government companies. Government companies have been given a State guarantee in a limited number of cases only, where special or extreme circumstances occur. The support was provided by means of state guarantee, state loans or postponement of payment of existing loans against extra shares, or concession of loans.

One example of a state guarantee occurs in the case of the Ashra Israel Export Insurance Corp. Ltd. ("Ashra"). Worldwide, companies that insure foreign trade risks deriving from medium and long-term credit risks in export transactions against commercial and political risks, receive backing from the State in which they operate. Examples are OPIC in the USA, ECGD in the UK and EKF in Denmark. In Israel, Ashra is the government company that insures foreign trade risks deriving from medium and long-term credit risks in Israeli export transactions, against commercial and political risks. Within the framework of this activity, the company benefits from a full State guarantee amounting to USD 700 million.

Source: Submission by Israeli authorities in response to OECD questionnaire.

Table 8. Conditions for explicit government guarantees

Canada	SOEs are considered either agents or non-agents of the Crown. By law, the government is liable for the actions and decisions of SOEs that are agents of the Crown, which applies to 28 SOEs. Any contract or loan entered into by an agent of the Crown effectively binds the Crown to the contract or loan. As a result, the state is effectively a guarantor of the loans of Crown agent SOEs, although legally speaking there is no contractual engagement between the state and commercial lenders to guarantee their loans. There are no conditions attached to the effective "guarantees" that agents of the Crown may benefit from.
Chile	SOEs can benefit from state guarantees on commercial debt in order to fulfil public policy objectives. The Ministry of Finance is responsible for allocating guarantees to its portfolio of SOEs. Dedicated legislation fixes an upward limit to the total amount of SOE debt for which the state can act as guarantor.
Germany	The rail company Deutsche Bahn benefits from an implicit state guarantee on its debt and has received interest-free loans from the central government, in line with the infrastructural responsibility of the Federal Republic of Germany stipulated in section 87e of the basic law. As a general rule, SOEs with sectoral policy objectives may also benefit from state guarantees on debt.
Israel	While the state does not as a general rule guarantee the commercial debt of SOEs, guarantees have been extended to SOEs in a limited number of cases. The Israel Export Insurance Corporation Ltd. (Ashra), which insures companies against commercial and political risks associated with foreign trade, benefits from a standing state guarantee of USD 700 million. The Israel Electric Corporation Ltd. received an exceptional government guarantee when the company's foreign natural gas provisions were interrupted (see Box 6).
Japan	State-owned airport companies can benefit from an explicit state guarantee and advantageous financing terms.
Netherlands	A minority of specific SOEs benefit from an explicit state guarantee on debt, and these are the state-owned financial institutions and Dutch Railways. In the latter case, Dutch Railways is required to pay a commercial fee for the guarantee.
New Zealand	The majority of SOEs are expected to obtain debt financing on the commercial marketplace and required to explicitly stipulate that their debt does not carry a governmental guarantee. However, NZ Railways Corporation (KiwiRail) is an exception; it is a statutory corporation whose original underpinning legislation stipulated that debt required Ministry of Finance approval and could benefit from an explicit state guarantee. The law has since been revised, but the explicit guarantee still applies to previously contracted debt.
Norway	In line with the EEA (European Economic Area) Agreement, the state is by law not permitted to issue government guarantees on commercial debt and companies are required to obtain debt financing in the marketplace.
Poland	SOEs are able to benefit from state guarantees, based on the Act of 8 May 1997, which lays out conditions that allow the Treasury to grant guarantees to both state-owned and privately-owned companies. No information was available on the procedures or criteria relating to the provision of such state guarantees.

Table 8. **Conditions for explicit government guarantees** (continued)

Slovenia	SOEs are excluded from the Act on Guarantees of the Republic of Slovenia, which establishes the general conditions for companies to benefit from state guarantees. However, SOE can benefit from state guarantees via special guarantee laws and when the activities for which the guarantee is requested are deemed to be in the public interest. Examples of activities deemed to be in the public interest include the provision of transportation infrastructure (railways, highways) and financing (export banks and development banks).
Switzerland	There are no explicit guarantees for SOEs' commercial debt. However, the federal state issues letters of guarantee for sub-national railway companies in order to ensure their rates are consistent with those faced by Swiss Federal Railways SBB, which benefits from EUROFIMA rates.

Source: Submissions by national authorities in response to OECD questionnaire.

Table 9. **Conditions for SOE debt financing from government agencies**

Australia	Australia's competitive neutrality policy requires government businesses to adjust their cost base, and therefore prices, where they borrow money at the rate that reflects the credit risk of the Australian Government as a whole rather than a rate reflecting the credit risk of the business activity being undertaken. For SOEs borrowing from the government at non-commercial rates, debt neutrality adjustments are incorporated in the cost of debt (e.g. Defence Housing Australia is subject to a debt neutrality charge equal to a margin above the 10-year treasury bond rate).
Canada	Four SOEs are able to borrow directly from the government: Canada Mortgage and Housing Corporation, the Business Development Bank of Canada, Farm Credit Canada and the Canadian Dairy Commission. In these cases, there is no mechanism to ensure market consistency of loan terms; loans are subject to an interest rate equal to the cost of debt for the government.
Estonia	The majority of SOEs access debt financing on the marketplace. Exceptionally, state treasury loans were granted to Estonian Air in 2012 and Tallinna Port in 2009. Guidelines elaborated by the authorities stipulate that treasury loans can only be provided in cases of restricted commercial financing, e.g. a financial crisis, and upon demonstration that such financing can improve the company's performance. For treasury loans, the interest rate applied is based on the cost of capital for the state and a risk premium. SOE borrowers are encouraged to rapidly refinance through a commercial bank.
Hungary	While SOEs access the majority of debt financing on the marketplace, credit can in some cases obtained from the state. Its terms are subject to a review on market consistency by the State Aid Monitoring Office under EU standards.
Poland	The Minister of Treasury can grant SOEs public aid loans pursuant to a regulation on the rescue and restructuring of companies that was passed in 2011.

Table 9. **Conditions for SOE debt financing from government agencies** (continued)

Switzerland	While most SOEs access debt financing uniquely on the marketplace, Swiss Federal Railways SBB is an exception and can obtain loans from the treasury, which must be provided on market terms and may not exceed a pre-defined upper limit. Loan terms are a combination of the interest rate the state pays on its debt and a commercial fee charged to the SOE.
United Kingdom	The majority of SOEs obtain all of their debt financing either from the National Loans Fund or via the relevant shareholding department, in agreement with the treasury. Government loans require the presentation of a solid business plan which is subject to scrutiny by the shareholding department. For commercial SOEs that compete with private sector actors, loans from the National Loan Fund are subject to specific arrangements to ensure market consistent borrowing terms.

Source: Submissions by national authorities in response to OECD questionnaire.

4. Remaining challenges to competitive neutrality

A main finding from this report's stock-taking of national practices is that authorities in an average OECD country approach the issue of financing SOE operations with quite a high degree of professionalism. This contrasts with the experience of previous decades where SOEs were sometimes perceived either as "fiscal sinks" where hidden reserves could be parked, or "milk cows" to be exploited as a source of revenue to the point where their viability was seriously imperilled. This confirms a tendency explored by other publications by the Working Party (e.g. OECD, 2011) which have found that recent SOE reform has largely moved national practices closer to commonly agreed standards. However, it bears mentioning that anecdotal evidence abounds that practices pursued in enterprises controlled by sub-national levels of government in a number of OECD countries are far less progressed with their reform processes.

While the state ownership functions and individual SOEs may have become more "professional" and approached themselves to the practices in similar private enterprises, it is also fair to say that no single model has emerged. For instance, only a minority of OECD's member countries systematically engage in assessments of the appropriateness of SOEs' capital structure, but a significant additional number make implicit decisions to a similar effect through evolving rate-of-return requirements and dividend policies. Only a minority of countries make such decisions purely or largely on an ad-hoc basis. Most OECD governments retain the option of redressing the capital/debt balance of SOEs through the infusion of direct subsidies, but – inter alia reflecting the strictures of WTO rules and, in many cases also the EU Single Market – generally reserve this for SOEs that are assigned special public policy obligations.

Most OECD area governments retain the option of recapitalising their SOEs – through share issuance, debt-equity swaps or, in the case of wholly-owned enterprises, infusion of funds. In most cases this is apparently motivated by a need to fund additional capital formation by the SOE, but it may also reflect a need to address excessive leverage (e.g. in case of initially too optimistic profit expectations and dividend policies) or, in rarer cases, to stave off a threatening corporate failure.

State-owned enterprises in OECD countries generally obtain most of their debt finance from privately owned banks. Only some of the largest and most commercially operating companies issue tradable debt, and quite a few SOEs that could profitably do so seem to refrain because of concerns about the additional corporate governance and reporting requirements that this entails under securities rules. Conversely, some of the SOEs that have issued corporate bonds have done so specifically in connection with their owners' efforts to upgrade their governance. Some governments which make treasury loans available to SOEs (one even demands that SOEs raise debt finance only from the national Treasury) generally have rules in place to ensure market consistency of interest rates and conditions. Loans from state-owned financial institutions are generally available only under circumstances (e.g. export credit; development banks) where a certain subsidisation would be available to private companies in like circumstances. The conclusion therefore offers itself that SOEs in OECD countries generally borrow money on market-consistent terms.

The relative sound financial operating environment, including recent improvements, should however not lead to the conclusion that there are no remaining problems to be addressed. Again, from a competitive neutrality perspective some areas of concerns offer themselves. As in other cases this is particularly the case in SOEs that pursue both commercial and non-commercial priorities and are unable to account separately for the cost structures of the two sets of activities. Based on the findings of the present report they include:

- *Rates of return.* Perhaps the most important outstanding issue is the trouble with monitoring whether rate-of-return requirements imposed on SOEs are comparable with those demanded of private enterprises. Even in an ideal situation this would be problematic since rate-of-return measures necessarily need to be considered over a long time span. In the case of OECD countries' current practices it is potentially more serious as a majority of countries, by their own admission, do not impose rate-of-return requirements on their wholly state-owned enterprises. Some governments moreover appear to compensate SOEs for having to assume public policy functions (rather than through a carefully calibrated subsidy) by negotiating relatively low rates-of-return, effectively providing these enterprises with a perverse incentive to expand in the market place.
- *Recapitalisation.* The conditions on which recapitalisation is offered to (wholly-owned) SOEs is notoriously difficult to assess empirically. Some disciplines on the conditions of recapitalisation exist, including the EU Commission's demand that practices may

not differ from private enterprises in like circumstances. However, such requirements can be difficult to enforce in practice, including in cases where recapitalisation efforts may be conducted in unison with private investors acting in concert with governments.

- *Perceived guarantees.* Whereas actual lending to SOEs seems to take place largely on market terms, commercial lenders may well perceive state-owned enterprises as more credit-worthy than their private competitors. Relatively few governments offer explicit guarantees to SOEs, but credit ratings and other indicators suggest that financial market participants in many cases perceive implicit guarantees. The only OECD country having in place measures to neutralise this competitive advantage is Australia with its "debt neutrality payments" from SOEs to the national treasury.

Notes

1. The information about the Japanese SOE sector in this report covers only state-owned airport and expressway companies.

2. Questionnaire response from Lithuania reports that fully incorporated SOEs are operated either as limited liability companies (under ordinary company law) or as "state enterprises" (under a dedicated Law on State and Municipal Enterprises). For both legal forms, the underpinning legislation stipulates that capital structure decisions are the purview of SOE boards and/or CEOs.

3. Questionnaire response from United Kingdom excluded a number of SOEs considered outside the scope of the exercise, notably Royal Mail and Channel 4, owing to the fact that these companies have been given a high level of autonomy to lead business strategy and operations. In these cases, the government has "consent" powers in capital structure decisions but does not play a strong oversight role.

4. The state ownership policy of the Netherlands is under revision and expected to be finalised in 2013. According to questionnaire responses, the revised policy will include explicit guidelines for calculating SOEs' cost of capital, using the Capital Asset Pricing Model.

5. In Ireland, while the authorities do not set rate-of-return requirements for the general SOE sector, some SOEs in regulated industries (electricity, gas and infrastructure) face rate-of-return requirements established by an independent regulator. Similarly, in Israel, the Government Companies Authority does not define explicit rate-of-return or financial targets, except in regulated sectors where tariffs are established by regulation. Questionnaire response from Ireland reports that the authorities are currently developing a mechanism to communicate more explicit expectations on SOEs' rates of return, which will be based on total shareholder return and involve industry peer comparisons.

6. In the Netherlands, in addition to the target credit rating, the authorities also communicate the expectation that SOE dividends amount to at least 40% of net income.

7. Israel and Slovenia report that extraordinary dividends, although rare, can occur in response to state budgetary needs.

8. For additional information, see OECD (2012), "Competitive Neutrality: National Practices", OECD, Paris. See also http://ec.europa.eu/competition/state_aid/legislation/sgei.html.

9. State support can also take the form of regulatory advantages conferred to SOEs, which is not the subject of the report. For a more detailed discussion of these and other competitive neutrality challenges and remedies in OECD countries, see OECD (2012), Competitive Neutrality: Maintaining a Level Playing Field Between Public and Private Businesses, OECD Paris.

10. According to questionnaire response from Canada, all SOEs ("Crown Corporations") are established for the purpose of fulfilling a public policy objective.

11. For the purpose of this report, recapitalisation comprises both capital injections and capital transfers, as defined by the Eurostat Manual on Government Deficit and Debt (Eurostat 2012). According to Eurostat, a capital injection is understood to denote a provision of funds in exchange for a corresponding increase in the investor's equity stake, while a capital transfer is understood to denote a provision of funds without an exchange of anything of corresponding value.

12. Leveraged recapitalisations are theoretically possible for SOEs, but questionnaire responses did not provide any information indicating the actual use of this practice by SOEs.

13. Questionnaire response for Canada indicated that information on SOE recapitalisations from the public budget was not available, and for Ireland that this was not applicable.

14. However, governments subject to EU (and EEA) rules are subject to rules aimed at ensuring that they do not provide capital unless private investors in like circumstances would have acted similarly.

15. In Hungary, the cost of equity capital for SOE recapitalisations is subject to a review by the State Aid Monitoring Office in accordance with EU regulations.

16. Under the Australian Corporations Act 2001, companies that issue bonds are considered "disclosing entities", and are thereby subject to enhanced information disclosure requirements that exceed the information disclosure requirements on SOEs laid out in the Government Business Enterprise Guidelines.

17. SOEs can notably receive loans from KfW (state-owned development bank), as can privately-owned companies. Questionnaire response from Germany indicates that SOEs do not face advantageous terms when accessing loans from KfW.

18. According to the submission by the Australian authorities in the context of the 2012 OECD report on "Competitive Neutrality: National Practices".

Bibliography

Canada Post (2012), Annual Report 2012, *http://www.canadapost.ca/cpo/mc/assets/pdf/aboutus/annualreport/2012_AR_complete_en.pdf*, accessed August 2013.

Commonwealth of Australia (2011), Department of Finance and Deregulation, "Commonwealth Government Business Enterprise Governance and Oversight Guidelines", http://www.finance.gov.au/publications/governance-arrangements/, accessed July 2013.

Commonwealth of Australia (2004), Department of Finance and Administration, "Australian Competitive Neutrality Guidelines for Managers", *http://www.finance.gov.au/publications/finance-circulars/2004/docs/AGCN_guide_v4.pdf*.

Commonwealth Competitive Neutrality Complaints Office (1998), "Rate-of-return Issues", CCNCO Research Paper, *http://www.pc.gov.au/__data/assets/pdf_file/0014/5414/cnror.pdf*, accessed June 2013.

Department of Finance of Canada, "Minister of Finance Financial Risk Management Guidelines for Crown Corporations", *http://www.fin.gc.ca/activty/pubs/frmcc-grfsc-eng.asp*, accessed August 2012.

Department of Finance of Ireland, "Code of Practice for Governance of State Bodies", *http://govacc.per.gov.ie/files/2012/03/codepractstatebod09.pdf*, accessed July 2013.

Eurostat (2012), Manual on Government Deficit and Debt. Implementation of ESA95, Eurostat Methodologies and Working Papers. Publications Office of the European Union, Luxembourg, *http://epp.eurostat.ec.europa.eu/cache/ITY_OFFPUB/KS-RA-12-003/EN/KS-RA-12-003-EN.PDF*.

Government Offices of Sweden (2011), "Annual Report State-owned Companies", *http://www.government.se/content/1/c6/20/44/34/bd7320d8.pdf*, accessed July 2013.

New Zealand Treasury (2012), "Owner's Expectations Manual. Crown Ownership Monitoring Unit", *http://www.comu.govt.nz/publications/guidance/owners-expectations-manual/*, accessed June 2013.

New Zealand Treasury (1997), "Estimating the Cost of Capital for Crown Entities and State-Owned Enterprises: A Handbook Prepared for the Treasury", *http://www.treasury.govt.nz/publications/guidance/reporting/costcapital/costcapital-oct97.pdf*, accessed June 2013.

New Zealand Parliamentary Counsel Office (1986), "State-Owned Enterprises Act 1986", http://www.legislation.govt.nz/act/public/1986/0124/latest/DLM97377.html, accessed June 2013.

OECD (2012), Competitive Neutrality: National Practices, Paris.

OECD (2011), Corporate Governance of State-Owned Enterprises: Change and Reform in OECD Countries since 2005, Paris.

OECD (2005), OECD Guidelines on Corporate Governance of State-Owned Enterprises, Paris.

The State of Queensland (2006), "Government Owned Corporations – Cost of Capital Principles", *http://www.ogoc.qld.gov.au/goc-policies/cost-of-capital-principles-paper-feb-06.pdf*, accessed June 2013.

Annex: Recent cases of SOE establishment

13 countries report having recently established SOEs, or acquired ownership in private companies. The details of these instances, including the reported rationale behind them, are summarised below.

- In Australia, two Government Business Enterprises recently acquired shares in private companies for primarily commercial reasons. In 2012, Australia Post finalised the acquisition of Star Track Express, a national road freight company (Australia Post already owned 50% of the company in a joint venture with Qantas since 2003). In 2010, Medibank acquired McKesson Asia-Pacific, a health services company specialising in tele-health and virtual healthcare.
- In Canada, five SOEs have been established since 2008: Canada Employment Insurance Financing Board (2008, human resources and skills development); PPP Canada (2008, finance); Canadian Museum for Human Rights (2008, Canadian heritage); Canadian Museum of Immigration at Pier 1(2010, Canadian heritage); and Windsor-Detroit Bridge Authority (2010, transportation and infrastructure). In addition, during the financial crisis, the government acquired equity shares in the automobile companies General Motors and Chrysler in return for temporary capital injections. In November 2012, the government sold 20% of its General Motors shares. In 2011, the government relinquished all equity stakes in Chrysler.
- In Estonia, a few notable SOE establishments have taken place since 2009. In 2012, 5 state-owned road maintenance companies were merged into one central SOE (AS Eesti Teed) to improve the quality of road maintenance in the country (both on the operational level and via increased investment capacity to purchase technology for improved service delivery). In 2012, the two subsidiaries of Estonian Railways (AS Eesti Raudtee, responsible for infrastructure activities and AS EVR Cargo, responsible for cargo activities) became two separate SOEs and the parent company was dissolved. The subsidiaries were originally established in 2009 to structurally

separate Estonian Railways' infrastructure and cargo activities. In 2010, the electricity distribution company AS Elering, originally a subsidiary of state-owned electricity production company AS Eesti Energia, became an independent entity to promote competition between electricity production companies.

- In Finland, some new SOEs have been established recently, either to create a new company from a demerged part of an existing SOE or due to the incorporation of a state-owned statutory or quasi corporation. There are no explicit policies in place regarding the rationale for establishing new SOEs.
- In Hungary, the authorities have recently established new SOEs. The reported motivation behind state ownership of these enterprises is that their primary activities are non-commercial. Further details on these SOEs were not reported. The state also acquired ownership in two private companies considered vital to the Hungarian economy. In these cases, independent evaluations of the companies' financial plans formed the basis for ensuring that the investment was made according to market standards.
- In Ireland, the authorities are currently in the process of establishing a state-owned water utility, which will take over the water functions of 34 local authorities.
- In Israel, the authorities have recently established a few new SOEs and SOE subsidiaries, and there have also been recent cases of SOEs acquiring partial or full ownership of private companies. Responses indicate that the acquisition of ownership by SOEs in private companies is primarily motivated by commercial reasons, while a government decision to establish an SOE is primarily motivated by public interest considerations or the presence of market failures. (Ownership acquisition by SOEs is subject to government approval based on the Government Company Authority's opinion, which takes into consideration both commercial priorities and consistency with the SOE's objectives.)
- In Lithuania, the only reported cases of new SOE establishment involved the creation of two new companies through mergers of smaller entities operating in the same sector.
- In the Netherlands, the only reported cases of recent SOE establishment involved the acquisition of ownership in the former SOEs of the islands of Sint Maarten, Saba and St. Eustacius when they became municipalities of the Netherlands. Responses indicate that in general the decision to establish new SOEs is primarily

motivated by: the necessity to contain a financial crisis; the establishment of large infrastructural projects that cannot be executed by the private market; the maintenance of monopolies for vital infrastructure; and a situation where a company's sole clients are public entities. (Responses also reported the temporary state acquisition of ownership in three financial institutions. These cases have been excluded because practices regarding state-owned financial institutions were not the primary objective of the exercise.)

- In New Zealand, two new SOEs were recently established, both with primarily public policy objectives. Southern Response Earthquake Services Ltd. was established following the 2011 Canterbury earthquakes to facilitate the treatment of insurance claims. It is expected to be a time-limited entity. Crown Fibre Holdings Ltd (CFH) was established in 2009 to co-ordinate the Crown's investment to establish a nation-wide ultrafast broadband network. CFH's role is to select private sector partners and manage co-investment to implement the network by 2019. CFH has been designated as a public benefit entity as it aims to provide services to the public rather than to make a financial return. As such there is no expectation that it will pay dividends to the Crown.
- In Norway, there are few recent examples of SOE establishment. Eksportkreditt Norge AS (Export Credit Norway) was established on 25 June 2012 to provide state-subsidised loans for export financing. The terms of these CIRR (Commercial Interest Reference Rate) loans are in compliance with the OECD "Arrangement on Officially Supported Export Credits".
- In Slovenia, the authorities are currently in the process of establishing a state-owned "bad bank" to purchase non-performing loans from private banks. The bank could have mixed ownership in the future.
- In Sweden, 12 new SOEs have been established in the last five years, the majority of which are commercial entities that had previously not been incorporated. Among these SOEs, two are in the financial sector, one focuses on research and development, and three have been established as part of the de-monopolisation of the pharmacy industry.
- In the United Kingdom, one SOE, the Green Investment Bank, was established in 2012 to stimulate investment in sustainable energy infrastructure projects. In addition, the Ordnance Survey took ownership of a private entity to fulfil certainly public policy

objectives (this was reportedly a small transaction). The government is currently planning to establish a British Business Bank to promote investment in small and medium-sized enterprises (SMEs), expected to be operational in 2014.

ORGANISATION FOR ECONOMIC CO-OPERATION AND DEVELOPMENT

The OECD is a unique forum where governments work together to address the economic, social and environmental challenges of globalisation. The OECD is also at the forefront of efforts to understand and to help governments respond to new developments and concerns, such as corporate governance, the information economy and the challenges of an ageing population. The Organisation provides a setting where governments can compare policy experiences, seek answers to common problems, identify good practice and work to co-ordinate domestic and international policies.

The OECD member countries are: Australia, Austria, Belgium, Canada, Chile, the Czech Republic, Denmark, Estonia, Finland, France, Germany, Greece, Hungary, Iceland, Ireland, Israel, Italy, Japan, Korea, Luxembourg, Mexico, the Netherlands, New Zealand, Norway, Poland, Portugal, the Slovak Republic, Slovenia, Spain, Sweden, Switzerland, Turkey, the United Kingdom and the United States. The European Union takes part in the work of the OECD.

OECD Publishing disseminates widely the results of the Organisation's statistics gathering and research on economic, social and environmental issues, as well as the conventions, guidelines and standards agreed by its members.

Made in the USA
Las Vegas, NV
21 October 2024

10198544R00050